SpringerWienNewYork

Housing Density

**Department for
Building Construction
and Design – HB2**
Institute of Architecture
and Design
Vienna University
of Technology
Editor

2012

SpringerWienNewYork

Housing Density

Published by
Vienna University of Technology
Institute of Architecture and Design
Department for Building Construction
and Design – HB2
Gerhard Steixner
Head of department
T +43 / 1 / 588 01 270 26
http://www.hb2.tuwien.ac.at

Editorial work
Gerhard Steixner
Polina Petrova
Laura Hannappel
Linda Rukschcio
Vera Kumer

Translation
Lucie Motloch

Proofreading
Christoph von Pohl

Graphic design
Büro Ferkl

Print
Rema Print, Vienna

Copyright
authors, architects, students,
photographers

© 2012, Department for Building
Construction and Design – HB2
Vienna University of Technology /
Springer-Verlag, Wien

Printed in Austria

SpringerWienNewYork is a part of
Springer Science + Business Media
www.springer.at

Printed on acid-free and chlorine-free
bleached paper

SPIN: 80015906

One volume with numerous color and
black-and-white illustrations.

Library of Congress Control Number:
2011 944 827

ISBN 978-3-7091-0358-6
SpringerWienNewYork

Content

Floor Space Index 0.32 0.50 0.65

Project	**BBQ Village**	**Con[Trans]**	**Living Watzespitze**
Students	Laura Untertrifaller	Markus Göschl Alena Preldzic	Rebecca Bremer Nicole Neumayr
Instructor	Adele J. Gindlstrasser	Ulrike Hausdorf	Silvia Boday
Page	41	51	61

Projects

1.00   **1.10**   **1.35**   **1.40**

   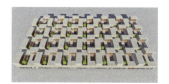

Courtyard House³   **Frame Story**   **The Inner World**

Fabian Antosch   Stefan Kristoffer   Emanuel Bührle   Eva Liisa Freuis-Manhart
Mauricio Duda   Susanne Mariacher   Melanie Hosner
                        Helene Schauer   Marius Nechville

Feria Gharakhanzadeh   Eva Češka   Martina Schöberl   Franziska Orso

Floor Space Index   1.65   1.70   2.50

Project	45.425277° / 12.327219°	Green Modules	Green Crossover
Students	Johannes Ritsch Sarah Wantoch	Viktoria Jiru Christian Daschek	Michael Strodl Maximilian Bauböck
Instructor	Kinayeh Geiswinkler-Aziz	Marlies Breuss	Ursula Schneider
Page	111	121	131

Projects

2.50   **2.70**   **2.82**   **3.00**

Housing Square

Bernd Hattinger
Fabian Lutter

Susanne Fritzer

141

Living Density

Annika Hillebrand
Philipp Rudigier

Maria Flöckner

151

Wood on a Higher Level

Isabell Ausserer
Alexandra Stummer

Katharina Fröch

161

Cracked

Emeli Steinbacher
Johann Szebeni

Gerda Maria Gerner

171

The Greatest Number
Gerhard Steixner

Housing construction for the greatest number is an important indicator of the social character of a society. Most people want to live in a single-family house. In the Netherlands, in England or in Japan, this wish is largely being taken into account. In contrast to these countries, the simple row house or the high-density, low-rise building has yet to be established as a cost-effective form of building in Austria. The percentage of apartment buildings in Austria is 60% and the construction costs are correspondingly higher than in the aforementioned countries.

A high percentage of the population not only has to be content with an unwelcome type of housing, but as a result of a low ownership rate also has to bear even higher expenses in the form of rising rents.

"Housing is a basic need for all, as well as an important social and economic matter of fact. A roof over one's head is expensive – the ownership of a house or an apartment can be expensive due to construction or purchase, but in the long term poses less of a financial burden; renting involves continually rising costs. In general, these costs belong to the most significant household expenditures."[1]

The result is a low level of housing and life satisfaction, both in absolute terms as well as in a Europe-wide comparison.[2] Declining birth rates, high social and healthcare costs, and the increased popularity of so-called protest parties[3] are a clear indication of the necessity for a paradigm shift when it comes to housing.

Repeated efforts since the First World War to achieve cost-effective, ecological and socially sustainable construction – and buildings to serve as examples thereof – show that the problem is not a lack of knowledge, but of competitive mechanisms and, because of other interests, a lack of will to implement this knowledge.

However, we as architects cannot bridge the gap between constructed reality and the users' desires on our own. Housing construction is urban development and therefore a category of the political.

After the First World War, Vienna's first city councilor for housing declared that, given the city's many tenement blocks from the "Gründerzeit"[4], only single-family houses would be built in the future.

Josef Frank and Adolf Loos were the protagonists of the Vienna Settlers' Movement which attempted to promote the incipient democratization of society in the area of public housing. Low development densities, spacious gardens and communal facilities such as swimming pools, kindergartens, libraries, laundry and healthcare facilities were characteristic features of the "superblocks"[5] of Red Vienna built in the thirties of the last century.

After the Second World War, Roland Rainer continued the efforts to provide livable housing. His writings[6] on housing issues laid the groundwork for the Europe-wide search for alternatives to the status quo in housing construction and urban development that resurfaced in the mid-sixties. New forms of urban housing[7] were developed as an answer to the perimeter block and the row house. High-density low-rise buildings and – in response to the call for higher density – terrace complexes

Karl Marx Hof
Vienna XIX, 1930, Karl Ehn
Housing units: 1382

Left

Housing Estate Hoffingergasse
Vienna XII, 1921, Josef Frank,
Erich Faber
Housing units: 284

were perceived as the ideal typologies of the time. Harry Glück's collaboration with the director of GESIBA[8] enabled him as one of only a few architects in Europe to realize this dream on a large scale.

His terrace complexes from the seventies and eighties of the last century today rank among those buildings with the highest level of housing satisfaction. With 14,000 housing units, he made a lasting contribution to Vienna's urban landscape.

With the help of the then-director of the *Neue Heimat* housing cooperative in Upper Austria, Roland Rainer was able to realize what – apart from three small housing estates – he had been denied in Vienna: his garden city Puchenau near Linz with nearly one thousand housing units. Today, Puchenau is considered a milestone in European housing construction.

This shows that architecture needs people with courage, architects as well as builders, politicians and cultural institutions who resist the entrenched forces with identity and idealistic values.

Viktor Hufnagl realized as many as 5,000 housing units for the city of Vienna. He developed different housing typologies of high quality in an experimental fashion. With his housing complex "Am Schöpfwerk", completed 1980 for eight thousand people, however, he could not build on the success of the Vienna Courtyards, which he tried to develop further.

The nearly double as high density[9] and approximately ten-fold larger size were parameters that demanded too much of both the underlying model and the innovative energy of the planner.

At the beginning of the nineties, a "New Gründerzeit"[10] was declared to deal with the expected immigration after the fall of the Berlin Wall and the opening of the borders to Eastern Europe. The urban planning department began to put more emphasis on full utilization of available building sites. New zoning instruments were generating higher site occupancy and floor space indices.

Puchenau Garden City
Puchenau, Upper Austria,
1963-2000, Roland Rainer
Housing units: 995

Housing Estate Am Schöpfwerk
Vienna XII, 1981, Viktor Hufnagl
Housing units: 2151
East elevation from the
school/church square

Left

Terrace Complex Inzersdorferstrasse
Vienna X, 1974, Harry Glück
Housing units: 222

Wienerberg City
Vienna X, 2001

Short-term capital and economic interests were taking priority over citizens' interests.

The density (Floor Space Index, FSI) resulting from the construction class and the site occupancy index.

Construction Class, Site Occupancy Index	Floor Space Index Mean Story Height 3.0
W I, 50%	1.75
W II, 50%	2.25
W III, 60%	3.3
W IV, 60%	4.5

The consequences of this housing policy are well known: the new urban expansion areas at the periphery are often characterized by high density, perimeter block development and a low proportion of open space coupled with long travel distances and a lack of infrastructure.

These disadvantages are often not compensated for by living in the countryside. Social segregation as a result of middle-class flight to the surrounding countryside[11] is another unwanted side effect.

Already in 1998, the then-Chancellor[12] of Austria wrote an essay titled "Humanes Wohnen als erklärtes Ziel" ["Humane housing as a declared goal"] urging that the same demands be met that have been raised repeatedly since the twenties: independent open spaces, gardens, proximity to recreational areas, guaranteed local amenities, possibilities for leisure activities, car-free residential areas, ecological construction, landscape-friendly types of housing, child-friendly.

The discrepancy between the wishes expressed and the constructed reality is obvious and urgently needs to be resolved. At present, a number of excellent architectural firms of the third and fourth generation are working on this problem. Their buildings and projects reflect the paradigm shift in "architecture" prescribed for housing construction in Vienna by the policy makers[13] of the time.

With their great commitment, knowledge and skill, many of them succeed in realizing livable buildings of high quality even within the tight constraints of rules, norms, economic and other utilization interests. The clients are aware of their responsibility concerning building culture and demonstrate "public interest" and "social commitment" in more than just their business documents. Typological innovations and new interpretations of known typologies are setting high standards in Vienna's housing construction.

As welcome as this development of the last ten years may sound, the contribution remains a very modest one in the thousandth range when measured against the total. Rather, the much-cited buildings actually obstruct the view onto the uniform chaos which lies behind them.

The key issues which policy makers have proclaimed since the beginning of the 21st century, such as the "New Settlers' Movement" [14], "social sustainability" [15] and recently also "civic participation" [16], are a clear indication of the deficits in housing construction and urban development today.

Now the time seems to be ripe for a new start for what would be the third attempt at democratization and ecologization of housing construction and urban development after the twenties and sixties of the last century.

Against the background of the current distribution debate, the responsible parties for urban planning and housing development can now - clearly acting in the interest of the common good - more determinedly set the course for the future of housing construction in Vienna.

The reform of subsidized housing construction, a forward-looking urban planning process with transparent zoning instruments as well as new participation, planning and contract award procedures are the prerequisites for the long-term realization of this goal. Moreover, general education and training are the basis for a qualified democratization of all areas of life.

Compact City
Vienna XXI, 2001, BUS architektur

Stacked Allotment Garden Settlement
Vienna XII, 2002, Helmut Wimmer

Housing Estate Orasteig
Vienna XXI, 2009, Walter Stelzhammer

Die Bremer Stadtmusikanten
Vienna XXII, 2010, ARTEC

The Faculty of Architecture of the Vienna University of Technology has for years enjoyed a steady increase in the number of students. We are therefore in a position to confront an ever growing number [17] of the next generation with key issues concerning the built and yet-to-be-built environment, with the aim of providing them with the competence that will enable them to participate actively and at eye level in the process of sustainable city inception.

In the "Design Studio Building Construction" [18], we regularly take up this opportunity with a variety of different issues. With housing density, we were able to confront almost four hundred young students in the 2009/2010 winter semester with the issue of housing in all its facets: Most people want to live in a single-family house. Is it possible to realize the qualities of single-family housing in high-density construction?

The aim was to develop building concepts [19] for different density requirements [20] for an abstract construction site of 5,000 m2 [21]. Apart from questions regarding construction methods, structures, materials and their joining, building services and building physics, the matter of floor space density and its implications for the development structure was an essential parameter of the task.

Introduced and accompanied by numerous lectures and study trips [22], the students developed approximately 180 projects on this topic in as many teams, in each case with a different focus.

The supervision of this great number was assigned exclusively to external instructors: fourteen young female architects [23] from all over Austria who, by themselves or in cooperation with partners, have already made or are making valuable contributions to different aspects of housing in theory or practice. Bearing in mind that the design studio was to be completed in the fifth semester, i.e. during the Bachelor program, the results were remarkable.

Fourteen works of students are presented, assigned to each of their respective instructors. They show that reducing the number of building regulation parameters can generate new, innovative settlement and building structures. They also show that typological diversity tends to decrease with increasing density, leading to familiar types of development such as slab block, perimeter block or point block.

The project "Cracked" by Emeli Steinbacher and Johann Szebeni with a floor space index of 3.0 extends this typological inventory while its terraced landscape promises good housing quality. The usage of the core zone and its natural lighting raises questions. High site coverage and low open space quality, however, would be the consequences of a high utilization of the building site.

With the project "The Inner World of the Outer World", Eva Liisa Freuis-Manhart succeeds in refining the low-rise housing development.

With a comparatively high density for this urban typology of 1.3, this project still retains the advantages of a single-family house with low construction and follow-up costs even compared to apartment buildings. A short construction time due to prefabrication and the passive use of solar power constitute another resource-saving potential.

Considering the results as a whole, an optimum for a balanced relationship between social, ecological and economical issues seems to be reached with a density of 1.4 FSI for residential areas.

The discussion begins with interviews[24] with Roland Rainer and Harry Glück, who were able to set milestones in European housing construction during the 1960s and 70s with similar demands on housing albeit with diametrically opposite concepts. The contributions by the architects and students will continue this discussion.

Terrace Complex Europan6
Vienna XI, 2010, PPAG

Sargfabrik
Vienna XIV, 1996,
BKK2, Johnny Winter

1 http://www.statistik.at/web_en/statistics/dwellings_buildings/index.html

2 SRZ (Stadt- und Regionalwissenschaftliches Zentrum): Wohnzufriedenheit und Wohnbedingungen in Österreich im europäischen Vergleich. [SRZ (Urban and Regional Research Institute): Housing satisfaction and housing conditions in Austria in a European comparison.] p. 2, May 2008

3 The occupants of those districts with the highest number of newly constructed buildings since 1990 clearly showed their dissatisfaction with this policy during the Vienna communal elections in 2010: In the 10th district of Vienna, the Social Democratic Party of Austria (SPÖ) lost 8.9%, in the 21st district 10.64% and in the 22nd 9.07%, and consequently the absolute majority in each case. [http://www.wien.gv.at/wahl/NET/GR101/GR101-109.htm]. Synthesis-Forschung: Wien – die städtische Bevölkerung und ihre Wohnversorgung – Städteberricht Wohnungspolitisches Monitoring [Synthesis Research: Vienna – the urban population and its housing supply – City report monitoring of housing policies] p. 11, November 2009

4 The floor space index of the tenement blocks built in Vienna during the years of rapid industrialization at the end of the 19th century is between 2.5 and 4 depending on the district. Werkstattbericht Nr.94 der Magistratsabteilung 18 – Stadtentwicklung und Stadtgestaltung. [Report No. 94, Municipal Department 18 – Urban Development and Planning] p. 100, Vienna 2008

5 The residential complex "Karl Marx Hof" for example has a site coverage of 18.4% and a floor space index of 1.1.

6 "Die Behausungsfrage" [The housing question] 1947; "Städtebauliche Prosa" [Urban developoment prose] 1948; "Ebenerdige Wohnhäuser" [Ground-level houses] 1948; "Die gegliederte und aufgelockerte Stadt" [The subdivided and broken-up city] in cooperation with Göderitz and Hoffmann, 1957

7 Hoffmann Ot, Repenthing Christoph: Neue urbane Wohnformen. Gartenhofhäuser, Teppichsiedlungen, Terrassenhäuser. [New forms of urban housing. Garden courtyard houses, low-rise housing complexes, terrace buildings] Ullstein, 1966

8 Non-profit housing estate and construction cooperative

9 At a site coverage of 54% the housing estate "Schöpfwerk" features a floor space index of 2.04.

10 Proclaimed by Hannes Swoboda, City Councillor for Urban Planning, Vienna 1988-1996

11 In the years from 2001 to 2008, the City of Vienna grew by 7.34% and the surrounding areas by 9.09%. PGO (Planungsgemeinschaft OST), H.Fassmann, P. Görgl, M. Helbich: Atlas der wachsenden Stadtregion, Materialband zum Modul 1 des Projekts „Strategien zur räumlichen Entwicklung der Ostregion (SRO)" [Planning Co-operation East. Atlas of the growing urban region, Material issue for Module 1 of the project "Strategies for spatial development of the eastern region"] p. 20

12 Viktor Klima, Federal Chancellor of Austria, 1997-2000

13 Werner Faymann, Executive City Councillor for Housing Construction and Urban Renewal 1994-1996, Executive City Councillor for Housing, Housing Construction and Urban Renewal 1996-2007

14 Rudi Schicker, City Councillor for Urban Planning, Traffic and Transport, 2001-2010

15 Michael Ludwig, Vice-Mayor and City Councillor for Housing, Housing Construction and Urban Renewal, 2007-2010, City Councillor for Housing, Housing Construction and Urban Renewal, since 2010

16 Maria Vassilakou, Vice-Mayor and City Councillor for Urban Planning, Traffic and Transport, Climate Protection, Energy and Public Participation, since 2010

17 New students of Architecture at the Vienna University of Technology: 776 in the year 2006, 1022 in the year 2009

18 A compulsory course of one semester as part of the Bachelor program

19 Not all instructors wanted to comply with this specification and either introduced the context (Venice, the mountains, the city, the hillside) or let the students choose the construction sites.

20 The floor space index of the submitted projects ranges between 0.3 and 3

21 50/100 m, vertical or horizontal

22 Excursions to the two opposite constrasts of density – the garden city Puchenau with a density of 0.627 (Rainer Roland, Amiras Nikolaus: Forschungsarbeit Gartenstadt Puchenau 2 [Research Work Garden City Puchenau 2], Architektur- und Baufachverlag Wien, 1984, p. 75) and the so-called Superblock Alt Erlaa with a density of 2.38. MA 18: Bebauungsformen und ihre städtebaulichen Kennwerte anhand von Wiener Beispielen [Municipal Department 18: Types of development and their urban development parameters based on examples from Vienna] p.15

23 Boday Silvia, Breuss Marlies, Češka Eva, Flöckner Maria, Fritzer Susanne, Fröch Katharina, Geiswinkler-Aziz Kinayeh, Gerner Gerda Maria, Gharakhanzadeh Feria, Gindlstrasser Adele, Hausdorf Ulrike, Orso Franziska, Schneider Ursula, Schöberl Martina

24 Excerpts from "Die Architektur und Ich" [Architecture and I], Steixner Gerhard, Welzig Maria, Böhlau Verlag, Wien 2003

Harry Glück

Harry Glück developed and realized – the latter as one of the few European architects since 1945 – a new concept for the construction of high-density housing. Glück thus positioned himself in a market niche and became one of the busiest Austrian (housing) architects. Although his concept is remarkable and has for decades been praised by building occupants, he has become something of a bogeyman for Austrian critics. For many years, Vienna's architecture scene was defined (or defined itself) in terms of form and reflection, effectively cutting out other, relevant issues. But this rejection was probably also due to the position of Glück's architectural firm as a planning office providing typical "commercial architecture" to insurance companies, banks, hotel chains, etc.

An interview with Harry Glück by Maria Welzig and Gerhard Steixner. We spoke with Harry Glück in July 1999 in his office in Vienna's Josefstadt district.

Steixner: How many homes have you designed?
Over the course of thirty years, I have been involved in the design of over 14,000 homes.

Welzig: Can you explain your housing concept to us?
Urban development and architecture today should no longer be projections of a hierarchical system but of a democratic mass society. A consumer society, if you will. The economic system that has prevailed – the capitalist market economy – is successful because it has as its basis a mass society that has the means to consume. If the majo-rity of people doesn't have money to spend, Chrysler won't sell any cars, Bosch no refrigerators and nobody buys a TV. Capitalism works because it feeds the cows it milks. Urban development in the 20th century thus faces a task which did not exist before. Before the year 1900, nobody cared about how the greatest number of people lived. All of a sudden, today's lower class – which became emancipated over the course of this century – is demanding the same standards as the privileged class. These demands are justified because they originate from our evolutionary programming and are basically the same ones which people who are privileged by wealth and/or power have always fulfilled for themselves. The Kennedys, for example, live today just as a Roman patrician or Chinese mandarin did 2,000 years ago. They live in contact with nature, with access to water, with a view if at all possible, with opportunities for recreational, physical and creative activities. This raises the question whether it is possible to build homes in such a way that the quality of living of the upper class can be made available to the masses on, so to speak, a democratic scale. That was the aim of my residential buildings, and it has worked relatively successfully.

Welzig: And how do your buildings work?
First of all, I showed how much more economically it can be done; then I made it clear that the amount saved should be invested in higher living quality. My idea of quality was not a more expensive façade, however, but optional functions. After all, housing is not about façades and baroque stair-cases, which you'll never find in social housing or

housing for the masses anyway. It will always be about functional options of which it can be hoped that that which is offered is also accepted. Finding these options is actually quite easy. Everybody would rather look at trees than at a fire wall, and most people would rather have a rooftop swimming pool than not. And most people would rather have a sauna in the house than not and would rather have a bad-weather playroom for the children and would rather have the garage underneath the house, no more than 40 meters to the elevator, no matter if it is for a disabled person or for a housewife coming home with the groceries and two children in tow. These are simple things. Everyone wants an apartment with an open space that is big enough for plants, and this open space for plants should be linked to the common green space, which is not a social green space of 5x10 m but a little park. It is possible to have terraces and loggias face such a park. This is the case in the low-energy house at Vienna's Handelskai. Just a few days ago, we received the final bill for this house from the developer. It shows that the gross building costs per square meter amounted to 15,200 Schilling (€ 1,105)[1]. With underground garages, with swimming pool, with 100% sheep wool carpets, with ceramic clinker bricks on all terraces and all footpaths, with expensive wooden windows, with heat recovery ventilation, etc. No other developer competition has ever come close to accomplishing this.

Welzig: The cost effectiveness of your buildings is mainly based on the central hallway access?
    Among other things.

Alt-Erlaa Housing Complex
Vienna XXIII, Austria
Start of planning: 1976
Completion: 1986
Housing units: 2900

Section

21

Welzig: In 1968, you began – at the same time as the neighboring Schöpfwerk[2] – to plan the towers of Alt-Erlaa.

First of all, the Alt-Erlaa buildings aren't towers; they are linear high-rise buildings whose lower 14 floors – which reach a height of 40 meters – are terraced in a parabolic shape. The aim was to create a properly functioning development with a large number of apartments and I was convinced this had to be realized using large green spaces despite the useful density. Alt-Erlaa proves that the population of a small town can be accommodated in a relatively small area, without being crowded, in a spacious environment, entirely without traffic, surrounded by a green space, with individual access that is convenient and barrier-free. The interior of the apartments cannot be seen from the outside, and all open to a 180 meter green space about the size of Vienna's Stadtpark between the Ring and the river Wien. The apartments have an absolutely unobstructed view to the south.

Steixner: You once called Alt-Erlaa the Versailles of democratic society.

I'm sure I didn't coin the phrase. But I am convinced that, in a democratic society, residential buildings have to be dominating elements in a city. In this sense, the comparison isn't all that wrong; but to say so of Alt-Erlaa of all places, just because it stands out as it does, is too obvious.

Welzig: At the end of the sixties, the terrace building was the ultimate answer to (housing) issues.

In many ways, it would still be so today.

Welzig: Then why is this form hardly being built anymore today?

There could be several reasons for this. At the time, opposition developed relatively quickly – it was strong, quite emotional and somehow directed against me personally. As a result, anything that was associated with me was not realized from the start – in order not to be considered partisan.

View from one of the terraces looking towards the building opposite.

Right: site, floor plan

Welzig: But you weren't the only one who proposed and built terrace buildings. At the exhibition "Neue städtische Wohnformen" ["New forms of urban housing"] organized by the Austrian Society for Architecture in 1967 and attended by almost all important Austrian architects, practically all the proposals were for terrace complexes. So what is there to be said against this form today?

You must have noticed that only the smallest part was realized. In order to build a terrace building in such a way that it does not cost more than an ordinary cube, two things are needed: first, the willingness to invest a considerably higher planning effort without being rewarded for it; and second, in all modesty, you also need the skill to be able to do it. Above all, there are no stereotype solutions. In my office, I have been dreaming the old architect's dream for 30 years; we put together a collection of details and floor plan types, and then we just reach into the drawer. Every architect tries this. As far as I know, everyone has failed, including me. If you react to the constraints of a limited site in an intelligent and responsible way, you will have to start from the beginning every time.

Steixner: And what is the secret that the buildings still look so good today after 20, 30 years, compared to others? Did you pay attention to durability and low maintenance in your specifications?

Not to the extent that I would have liked. For many projects, I was assigned partners for the final planning on whom I had only limited influence. The most important thing, I suppose, is that the occupants identify with my buildings.

Steixner: What is it that still motivates you, after having built so much already...

Even if it sounds silly: a certain missionary ambition to be of use to others within my range of possibilities. Around the middle of the 19th century, there was a socialist movement in England with the motto "The greatest good for the greatest number of people". This seems to me the basic premise of any political party, but it also is the basis of

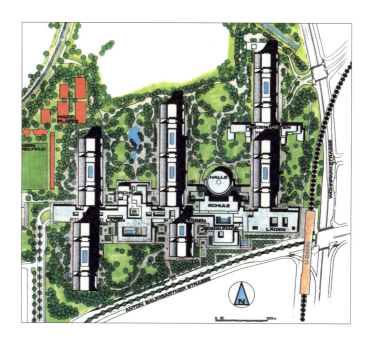

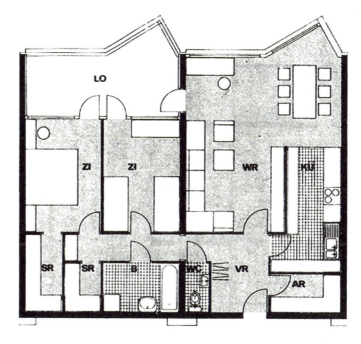

every humanitarian way of thinking. And of every Christian ethic, I would say. I therefore try to provide people with a better housing situation, a better living environment and the possibility to lead a satisfactory life with the potential for growth and development. I allow myself this, if you will, idealistic motive, I allow myself this luxury; actually, I believe that this luxury should be an obligation for anyone who possesses certain skills and abilities.

Welzig: Occupant satisfaction is reported to be very high in your buildings, as is the identification with the residential quarters. This is all the more remarkable in a housing complex the size of Alt-Erlaa. People have even set up their own television station there.

The social life there is, I think, unique in Vienna and in all of Europe. The clubs and events organized by the occupants themselves have been fully active for 20 years, despite – or perhaps because of – the generational change that has taken place since then. I suppose that there are not many newly created residential areas that have developed such a distinctive identity. You have to forget about the idea that you can convince people of something by resorting to entertainment hosts like in a Club Med. This may work for a certain period of time, but not over twenty years. The only thing that works over such long periods of time is that for which evolution has already programmed us. Alt-Erlaa offers – apart from certain basic options such as green spaces, peace and quiet, undisturbed living, open space for plants, rooftop swimming pools and a view – many rooms that are presented as boxes of bare concrete with electrical installations and mechanical ventilation. The residents themselves then organized parquet flooring for a dance club or seats and a stage for a children's theater, or shelves, tables and seating furniture for a reading room. At the end of the eighties, Bavarian Television came to Vienna in order to put on a defamatory campaign at Alt-Erlaa after already dedicating the first part of their film to the defamation of the International Building Exhibition (Interbau) in Berlin.

At Alt-Erlaa, however, the TV crew was steamrolled by the residents. And the result was, in contrast to Interbau, a half-hour commercial. The Austrian television, of course, did not show it, despite the fact that it was very flattering for Vienna.

Welzig: These days, common rooms in social housing are often left out for cost reasons. You used the dark areas of your terrace buildings for the common rooms. But what can be done to ensure that common rooms are used as such? Very often these things don't work as they are supposed to.

The building services at Alt-Erlaa are very good, and they are available onsite, but there is absolutely no… let's call it social animation. It isn't even necessary.

Welzig: But there are complexes in which a number of common rooms and so on were planned…

And they stand…

Welzig: …empty because…

…they are filled only with the resident janitor's furniture and snow tires because something that is absolutely necessary is missing, the "bonding situation", to use a term from the behavioral sciences. On the one hand, we are social beings who apparently find the deprivation of social contact to be very unpleasant; otherwise, we would not use solitary confinement as a form of punishment. But, on the other hand, the stranger we come across could also be an enemy. So we have developed certain rituals for coming together.

Welzig: And this social bond is the swimming pool.

In principle, it is the swimming pool. In small communities, it is the church, the shop, the tavern. Churches, shops and taverns exist in cities, too, but they no longer have the same function. So we need something else. The essence of a bonding situation is that it is frequented regularly and spontaneously. Everyone goes to the pool when it's sunny. You don't have to force anyone to go. Whether the weather is hot or you want to see the

Community rooftop pool

stars come out at night and watch the city lights… If this isn't your thing, you simply don't go up there and don't take part in these communal possibilities, but most people do. Many small things come into the picture here. People usually signal their status with their clothing. In the swimming pool area, nobody wears a tie. And if you meet someone at the pool for the third time in a row, well, then you say "Good evening" and the children already know each other from before, or…

Welzig: The settlement policy for Alt-Erlaa was quite different from the one at the municipal housing estates Trabrenngründe [3] or Schöpfwerk, wasn't it?

Not really. There was a study of income levels and the level of education at Alt-Erlaa and the nearby Schöpfwerk. Residents of Alt-Erlaa earned five percent more on average – that's not very much. About 25 percent of the residents of Alt-Erlaa receive housing subsidy, compared to 35 percent at Schöpfwerk. The class is certainly a somewhat higher one, but both correspond to the average population in municipal housing or housing cooperatives in Vienna.

Welzig: Twenty years ago, it was common knowledge that the soccer star Hans Krankl was moving to Alt-Erlaa…

At that time, he was still not very well known.

Welzig: Then his moving to Alt-Erlaa probably would not have been common knowledge. Celebrities living there must play a role for how people see themselves.

Do you think that the 10,000 people who live there are all soccer fans or support the local club Rapid Wien?

Steixner: You consider housing to be a product. It was once said that housing must not become a commodity, a slogan from the left, and now you are making a product which, pointedly said, is "luxury" on a democratic scale. How actually is this compat-

ible with your ideology as a person on the left?

Why should I make the product inferior if I can make it better? I previously cited the English proto-socialists – "The greatest good for the greatest number of people." If the economy and society continue to develop in the same way as in the last 50 years, I would – if I could plan housing 50 years from now – definitely make them more "luxurious" than today. The architect's job must be to use the means entrusted to him in the best way for the people they are intended for. And whether you call it a product or a good or whatever, it is just a play on words.

Steixner: It has been said that we've never had it as good as today… Why isn't this reflected in the quality of housing?

What I have done was to try to demonstrate that it doesn't have to be that way. Over the course of this century, the differences between the upper and lower classes have become gradual ones almost everywhere. The medical treatment a poor person receives today is in effect not any worse than what the rich get. Anybody with an average income can travel to Mauritius or Bali. The differences between the privileged and the lower classes have become gradual ones – except in housing. Here the differences are still fundamental ones. With my housing, I have tried to reduce them to gradual ones.

Steixner: If anything, housing today is even more cut back than twenty years ago. You can see it in your buildings too: this abundance of open spaces, boxes for plants and so on no longer exists on such a grand scale. Is there less money available or are there other reasons?

For a few years now, some public funding options have been available that you could only have dreamed of in the past. This means that cutbacks are happening due to ideological corsets and not because of money. For example, you can't get approval for the type of structure necessary for my concept.

Steixner: Well, those deep tracts...

If the land advisory board permits only two or three apartments per floor and dictates narrow structures, then there can not be a swimming pool, in this way they kill my whole idea. Central hallway access is a) not approved by the urban planning departments and b) declared not eligible for funding by the land advisory board. But this is the basic prerequisite for large green spaces.

Welzig: The central hallway access – the hallways with artificial lighting and apartments all facing to one side – is something your buildings have always been criticized for.

It is blatantly obvious that this argument is nonsense. No one can expect a studio apartment or a one- or two-room apartment to open up to more than one side. If I have a three- or four-room south-facing apartment, it never crosses anyone's mind to say that it should also face north. If you build housing with gallery access, as is the fashion today, then you have one half of a central hallway building in which the apartments also face to just one side.

Welzig: At least you don't have the dark areas.

I really would like to show you how dark they are, these famous dark areas. This is nonsense. Usually, the structure is spanned from the inside to the outside. This means that I have a little window – and a supporting beam, after all I've got to provide some support. The beam takes away the first 20 cm of light at the top. But if I choose the cross-wall construction method, then the window reaches to the ceiling and is much higher. If I additionally lower the parapet height to 60 cm, I get large windows that are perfectly capable of illuminating a room that is eight to nine meters deep and which helps connect the home with the green space. But now there is the famous argument of cross ventilation. To begin with, all our apartments are cross-ventilated from a hygienic perspective because the air inside is constantly vented. In hygienic terms, the constant ventilation of the interior in a central hallway building is much more effective than the kitchen or bathroom

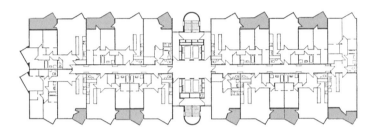

Floor plan with central
hallway access

transom windows in a gallery access building. Anyway, the idea of cross ventilation in apartments goes back to Friedrich Engels and his description of the conditions in back-to-back row houses with open cesspools in England's industrial cities in the mid-19th century. This is a historical prejudice. The alternative is the possibility of a functioning garage, building costs that are up to 20 percent lower, the option of having a roof garden or a swimming pool... now, if I compare this to the actual or alleged disadvantages, there is little room for an objective debate.

Welzig: The GESIBA housing cooperative with its director, Anton Muchna, was an understanding client.

That's true. But this understanding would have immediately come to an end had at some point something not worked. By the way, I've also built for other housing cooperatives which wanted the same thing as GESIBA. Others, in turn, who have hired me were interested only in economic efficiency.

Steixner: What do you think of the current housing construction activities in Vienna?

In such matters, I usually abide by the rules of professional conduct: I don't judge or label. Whether housing policy is successful, we've got elections for that. The politicians who determine the current policy of housing construction must also be held accountable for it. Either people are happy with it – in which case they will re-elect the city council which builds and finances housing, and the politicians will continue the same policy – or people are not happy with it and will express their discontent by voting for someone else. Xenophobia, too, flourishes on the basis of a prevailing atmosphere of discontent. At least this is what history teaches us. These democratic mechanisms, however, work very slowly. The housing and urban planning policy of the past 15 years is definitely not in line with the wishes of the people and of those seeking a place to live. This is so obvious that we can say it, because the people are leaving.

Physically, they are moving to suburban communities on the fringes; politically, they are turning to the protest parties.

Steixner: Do you see a connection here?

Partly yes. The housing situation is an essential part of life satisfaction, and in Vienna it is traditionally linked to politics. The housing and urban planning ideologies of the last few years, which, by the way, have been held by both major parties – perhaps a pact exists –, have quite obviously led to shortcomings in comparison with the previous pragmatic and more liberal policy.

Steixner: Do you really consider the housing and urban planning policy of the seventies more liberal than the current one?

The currently prevailing ideology defines the city as a structure where streets and open spaces are bounded by buildings, more or less densely speckled with restaurants, shops and places of leisure and entertainment, which is generally regarded as communicative urbanity. Nature comes into consideration only as a so-called "urban green". There surely is a target group for this concept of a city, but it is a minority, namely better-educated and higher-earning people who are starting their careers and are in the dating phase, as well as a certain intellectual bohemian scene. But the largest part of the population consists of, let's say, average or "normal" families, whose wishes and needs are focused on living in a green environment, on continuous contact with the neighbors, on leisure time which is preferably integrated into the housing situation. All in all, very basic demands. The expectations of the first group can in fact be met only in the city center. The other, larger group is simply offered the same type of city concept, but with strongly reduced functionality; you could almost say that this concept is imposed upon them for lack of alternatives. This arises from the erroneous assumption that streets and open spaces per se create a satisfactory urbanity, just as Jane Jacobs, some three decades ago, tried to sell her memoirs of a Mediterranean holiday as the essence of urban planning. A young family with children, however, has other needs. The result is the rejection of many of these apartments and continued suburbanization.

Steixner: In the nineties, the housing and urban planning policy of the city of Vienna overcame a taboo that had existed until then – the high-rise.

The expansion of high-rise buildings, at least in the case of residential buildings, cannot be justified on the grounds of urban planning or economic efficiency or any other arguments. The not even 90 apartments in the towers on Wagramer Straße, of which not more than half offer attractive views, lack any rationale from an urban planning perspective. Unless high-rises are some kind of compensation for phallic shortcomings. Thanks to the pharmaceutical industry, however, this no longer needs to be. This also reminds me of the fifties, when every small town mayor thought he could turn his one-horse town into a metropolis by building a high-rise. I don't think that the nineties have brought forth any noticeable progress in functionality, which includes spatial correlations. In many aspects, and this could also be argued in detail, we have regressed – and not just back to the fifties, but to the 19th century.

Welzig: In what sense?

In the sense that sites that would allow spacious solutions are being divided into lots as had been the case during the years of rapid industrialization at the end of the 19th century, resulting in the development of grid structures with perimeter blocks even at the city limits. Or that green spaces are not being planned as part of the residential environment but as scattered parks, just like in the 19th century. The city of the 21st century will have to reclaim the nature that was banished in the 19th century – otherwise the people will leave. This process is already under way. If cities in the traditional European sense want to survive, they will have to develop qualities that offer people the things they are looking for on the fringe.

1   Year of construction 1995

2   Housing estate of the city of Vienna in the 12th district, built in the 1960s based on plans by Viktor Hufnagl

3   Prefabricated housing estate in the 22nd district of Vienna, built in 1973-77 based on the design by architects Fritz Gerhard Mayr, Manfred Schuster and others

Roland Rainer

Roland Rainer in a nutshell: planner of indoor arenas, churches, houses and gardens; professor for housing, urban design and land use planning; head of master school for architecture; author, dogmatist, environmental activist. Much has been said about Roland Rainer already, but the significance of his work has not been appropriately acknowledged in Austria.

Going back to the roots of functionalism and anonymous construction, Rainer developed a radical social approach to building – an approach that is worlds away from what it means to be a celebrity architect today. Rainer preferred to reject commercialism posing as prestige and to concentrate his work on an overall concept focused on the basic necessities of life.

He seamlessly transferred to the present the ideas of modernism, whose main Viennese representatives he had known personally in the 1930s, and introduced issues such as nature conservation, cultural heritage management and ecology long before they became general concerns. He certainly was no anti-authoritarian; quite the contrary: in Austrian architecture, Roland Rainer is the great authority.

An interview with Roland Rainer by Maria Welzig and Gerhard Steixner. We spoke with Roland Rainer in 1999 in his office in Vienna's Hietzing district.

Steixner: In the early seventies, there was a student revolt against you at the Academy[1]. When I began my studies, in 1973, you could still see the traces on the walls – "Rainer-KZ[2] Puchenau" and so on. The spirit of that time was generally unfavorable to your concept of individual housing.

That was 1970/1971. I stuck to my position and tried to put the idea across to the young people in this city of old and new tenement blocks. And I think I succeeded – if you take a look at the projects those former students planned and built later as architects, the essence of their work was not very far from my own concepts. One of the "most revolutionary" was *Mark Mack*. Today he builds very beautiful, colorful, quite individual apartments and courtyard houses in Los Angeles. He has departed from his previous ambition to be revolutionary and social at all costs. He builds houses that people like to live in and which they hire him to build – which is just how I would do it.

Steixner: From that time until the beginning of the eighties, as I saw it, interest in the garden city concept and the ideas of modernism in general declined continuously. We spoke about that once, in 1984 I think it was. You seemed depressed. You had a long dry spell.

Yes, that may be true. Disappointing at that time was the lack of interest among the public, but also within professional circles. Postmodernism had fallen on fertile ground in Vienna, especially among all those architects who were satisfied to speak of "architecture" without really saying what they meant.

Steixner: If you look at Austrian publications, there is a striking lack of positive response. Where do you think this stems from?

The success of the dominating Holzmeister [3] group perhaps originated from the fact that Holzmeister's students could observe and learn social, tactical and political skills in addition to so-called architecture. My concern was to understand "architecture" as a whole, with all its relations to space, i.e. the scenic, urban, private and personal space; I was concerned with space in all its relations to time and its social, economic and cultural issues. Of course, the concepts I formulated and represented are not the typical Viennese version of contemporary architecture – the decorative and prestigious element is missing.

Welzig: In 1958, you became city planner of Vienna. After five years, you presented a comprehensive planning concept. It is hard to believe, but not one single high-density low-rise building came out of your tenure as city planner. Did you have any influence on the development of Südstadt, *which was planned by* Hubatsch/Kiener/Peichl *from 1958 onwards?*

This has to do with me only in so far as it reflected my views. Südstadt is situated outside the Vienna city limits. Peichl and I had worked together and, more importantly, Hubatsch was a friend of mine, and we often saw eye to eye. Peichl and Hubatsch could realize in Südstadt what I could not in Vienna.

Puchenau Garden City
Puchenau, Upper Austria
Start of planning: 1963
Completion: 2000
Housing units: 995

Puchenau Garden City
Semi-private access ways

Welzig: You say it is a basic mistake of Vienna's city planning that the surrounding area falls under another authority, that Vienna and Lower Austria are two separate political entities.

Hostile entities.

Welzig: Recently a study by the Austrian Conference on Spatial Planning showed that the demand for housing space is decreasing in Vienna while it is strongly on the rise in the surrounding region in Lower Austria.

What does it mean that people are leaving the capital and settling in the surrounding countryside? I had already observed and described this back in 1960. But was it debated, have there been attempts to take the logical next step from this basic fact? People are going to Lower Austria for what they want because they can't get it in Vienna. Vienna raised the maximum permissible construction height in such as way that it is becoming increasingly impossible to build single-family houses. The fact of people escaping to the surrounding countryside wouldn't be such a bad thing if Lower Austria had some urban planning concept; but instead of building a chain of satellite garden cities in these wonderful surroundings and establishing a connection to Vienna, as is the case in London, Lower Austria has for some inscrutable reason not had anything better to do than to build its own, completely unnecessary capital.

Welzig: We recently visited the Mauerberggasse housing estate that you had planned in the fifties. The quality of living is impressive.

And do you know how cheap those houses were? You wouldn't believe it, they were almost given away.

Welzig: We visited a house that has remained almost unchanged and in excellent condition. It is quite striking that many of your colleagues live there.

Nothing makes me happier than to see the people there happy. One of the most rewarding aspects of my work is walking through *Puchenau* and being stopped by one of the residents there. That has happened to me often. Once, I was walking through Puchenau with a Vienna city councilor, and an old lady came up to me and said: "Professor..." And I thought she wanted to complain about a leaking roof but she said: "I just wanted to tell you how happy we are here."

Steixner: But the Vienna reality seems downright opposed to your ideas.

Those aren't my ideas, they are the ideas of the garden city movement, ideals of an era that tried to think in a more cultivated and social manner. During the building boom in Vienna after 1918, Vienna's first city councilor for housing declared that, given the city's many tenement blocks, only single-family houses would be built in the future. That was the spirit of the time. As a student, I worked on the construction of the Lockerwiese housing estate, which belonged to a group of row-house estates that *Loos*[4] was in charge of. At the time, of course, Loos and *Frank*[5] were gods. The single-family house is the oldest urban housing type; all of Iran consists of courtyard houses and, until recently, the same could be said about China and the whole of the Western world, this is nothing new. In the Viennese district of *Hietzing*[6] and the area of *Lainz*[7], two-story single-family row houses are the norm. In Vorarlberg – where my mother is from – living in single-family houses is as natural as in the neighboring countries. Take a look at Holland and England! In England, it is taken for granted that everybody lives in a row house, it is an inherent part of democracy. In my opinion, progressive democracy is not possible without this conception. What is happening in Vienna today has nothing to do with democracy. 70 to 80 percent of the people would like to live in a single-family house. What percentage of single-family houses do we have in Vienna? Previously we had 5 percent – now, as a consequence of the new housing policy, we have about 4 percent.

Housing Estate Mauerberg
Start of planning: 1956
Completion: 1963
Housing units: 60

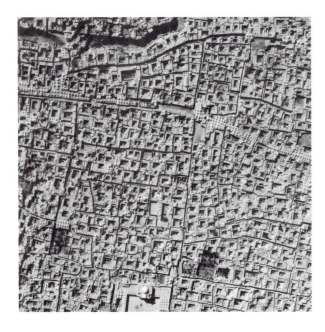

Isfahan, Iran
Aerial photo

Puchenau Garden City
Cultural center; courtyard in
front of kindergarten and
transition to residential area

*Welzig: One criticism of your urban planning and
housing concept is that it is anti-urban.*

I don't talk about that because it's just too ridi-
culous. Let me ask you this: was Pompeii anti-
urban? Is London anti-urban? Is all of Isfahan, all
of Beijing anti-urban? These people have no idea
what they are talking about. At the same time,
however, the public is being shown high-rise buildings made of corrugated sheet metal squeezed
between tiny green spaces and is told that Vienna
is "finally urban, finally a big city"!

*Welzig: Doesn't Puchenau lack possibilities for
communication for young people or people who
live alone? After all, you advocate the separation of use.*

I am in favor of separation of use when the different forms of use interfere with one another, but
there has to be a center for communal functions.
I don't think Puchenau can be an example for a
city because it is much too small. Moreover, one of
Puchenau's disadvantages is its proximity to Linz,
so that a substantial part of the social functions
is situated there. I believe that centers should be
dense, as dense as is necessary for their functions.
I have proposed district centers for Vienna as an
attempt at functional decentralization.

*Welzig: The district centers have indeed contri-
buted to the development of urban life in the
respective neighborhoods.*

There you are. I advocated decentralization
within the city; almost every district got its own
center, often developed out of the old village center.
The most well-known is Hietzing, where I had actually intended to establish a connection with the
Hietzing metro station but failed because it was not
possible to get around the garages of a hotel. In
a center, all the necessary public facilities have to
be combined. The surrounding housing development is built on another scale and is much less
dense. People should be able to live in peace and
quiet. A city is not an accumulation of buildings;
the important thing is not the building volume, but

the proper grouping of functions and the creation of living space.

Welzig: If it has to be multi-story, you have proposed south-facing windows for the buildings, arranged in parallel and separated by broad green belts. The terrace apartment complexes which were the focus of architect interest in the late sixties were not an issue for you?

No, because in a city as dense as Vienna I was in favor of the concept of breaking things up. I asked myself how I could best fulfill the people's desire for multifaceted relations to each other. In tenement blocks? Or in high-rise buildings? Do you think that people there talk a lot with each other? You can find everything about high-rise buildings in my book *Kriterien der wohnlichen Stadt (Criteria of a livable city)*. The book was published in 1978, but it is no shame if something that proves to be right is not entirely new. Surveys conducted in Puchenau have shown that the lower the houses, the better the contact and the higher they are, the worse. *Criteria of a livable city* shows a high-rise apartment building by Harry Glück, who, in spite of everything, always made an effort to consider the people. At the entrance to Alt-Erlaa, there are instructions on how to find a person's apartment. 1. Locate the party's number on the directory; 2. Enter the number on the keypad; 3. Signal sounds; 4. Call signal and repetition; 5. Entry error; 6. After establishing a connection you can speak; 7. The main gate is opened; 8. etc. etc. Imagine a little boy who wants to visit his friend: he is supposed to read all that. In Puchenau, he goes outside and immediately finds the others because people walk everywhere. Apart from the desire for communication in today's society, which constantly forces us to interaction with others, there also is a strong desire and need for retreat; in Puchenau, this is possible with just a few steps.

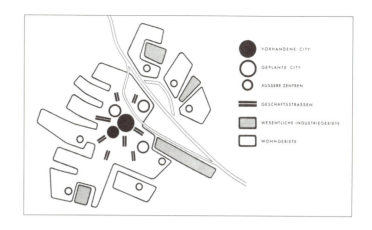

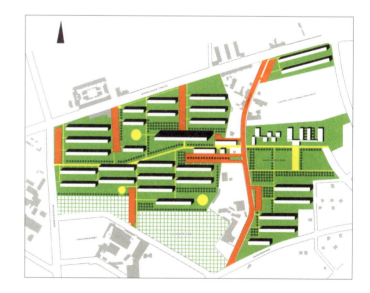

Vienna Planning Concept, 1961
Decentralized layout
Leopoldau development proposal

Puchenau Garden City

View over the private open space

Section

Steixner: House and garden are always a unity for you – entirely in the spirit of oriental and East Asian tradition.

Gardens are an environment where people and plants live together. They extend the housing space in the form of quiet, secluded courtyards where space, form, color and smell vary with the seasons. I really had my doubts if I shouldn't have become a biologist.

Welzig: You have stayed true to your housing ideal since the thirties. You have recently completed another atrium house estate in Vienna.

That would be the *Gartenheimstraße* in *Essling*. It was sold even before it was finished, unlike the triumphal high-rise buildings. As far as I am concerned, it is the best of all, the most economic and the most consistent. It is small, consisting of only eighty units. There was no more money left for walls around the courtyards, but I wanted to obtain a closed perimeter, so we chose a cheaper wooden fence: larch, untreated, and it is beautiful. Almost every week, people call me at my studio and ask: "Where can I get one of your houses?" I can only tell them that everything has already been sold.

Welzig: What about the Seenbezirk Linz-Pichling?

The Seenbezirk Linz-Pichling is a project for the expansion of Linz to the southeast for which I had to draw up a master plan. Intense surveys and debate among the inhabitants took place. Within a year the plan was unanimously accepted by both the authorities and the inhabitants. Then the architects Foster, Rogers and Herzog were invited for the final planning, which ended up looking completely different than the master plan, however. Contact with the people doing the final planning was not possible.

Welzig: You have been developing concepts for prefabricated houses since the fifties. Did you consider this for Puchenau?

Prefabricated houses were one of the first subjects I dealt with as an architect. As you may recall, I built the *Fertighaussiedlung Veitinger-*

gasse together with *Carl Auböck* and with an American expert as advisor in 1953. The estate of prefabricated houses, opposite the Wiener Werkbundsiedlung, is still occupied and has proved of value in every respect. It consists of ground-level wooden houses, with aluminum sliding roofs, built-in cupboards, prefabricated installation blocks and air heating. The wall constructions were built by Austrian firms according to their standard systems.
At the time, the public ridiculed the effort. At Puchenau, prefabrication was not an issue. But prefabricated houses are undoubtedly one of the industrial era's important contributions to the issue of housing; this has been known for a long time in the United States, in Sweden and in Finland and has been turned to an advantage there.

1   Academy of Fine Arts Vienna

2   Concentration camp

3   Clemens Holzmeister, 1886-1983, Austrian architect

4   Adolf Loos, 1870-1933, architect

5   Josef Frank, 1885-1967, architect

6   13th district of Vienna

7   Part of the district Hietzing

Projects

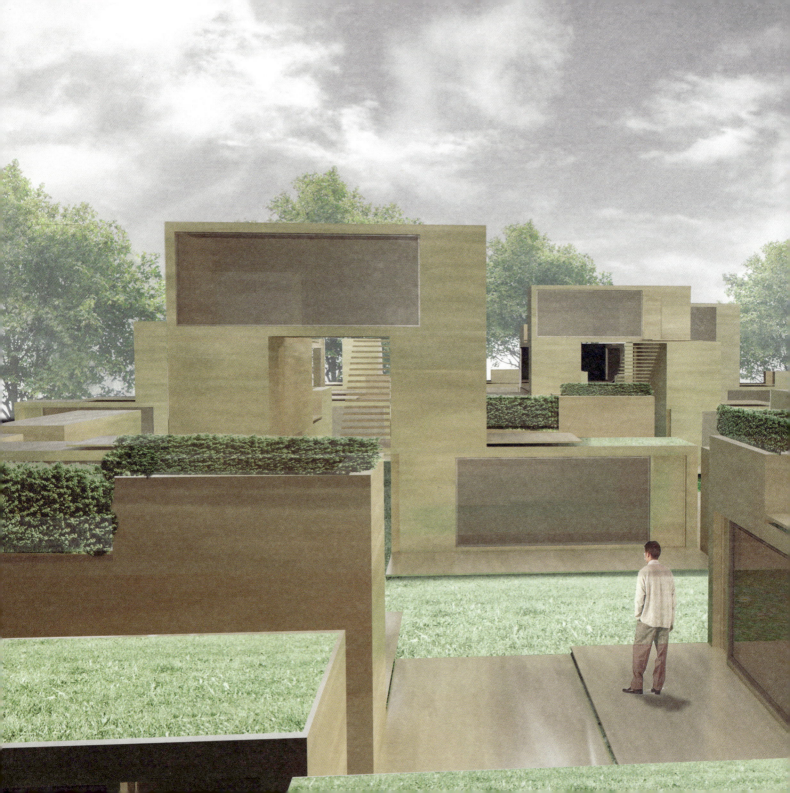

BBQ Village

Laura Untertrifaller
Student

Adele J. Gindlstrasser
Instructor

Floor space index   0.32

Plot area   5,000 m²
Gross floor area   1,600 m²
Total usable floor space   1,343 m²

Private open space   2,687 m²
Public space   70 m²

Housing units   79

Type of construction
Wooden solid construction

BBQ Village

The chosen site is located in Eibesbrunn in Lower Austria. Eibesbrunn is a village with predominantly small-scale development. The basic concept of my project is to adapt to the existing structural conditions. Therefore, the housing facility should not be an oversized complex. The first idea was to build a kind of stacked allotment garden settlement. However, it proved difficult to arrange the individual buildings in a way that would provide each unit with enough green open space on the roof of the next one.

As a consequence, a construction of more than three levels was hardly possible. The target group of BBQ village is mainly urban residents who like to get away from the city and go to the countryside in their spare time, make bike tours, work in the garden, barbecue, sunbathe and simply enjoy nature, as the village has beautiful surroundings with vineyards to offer.

The floor plans are designed to take up a minimum of space and at the same time guarantee an adequate living comfort. Each house has 17 m² of floor space. A multifunctional piece of furniture that serves as bed, study desk and dining table can be tipped up to create enough living space.

Bathroom and kitchen are reduced to a minimum. Special importance is attached to the terraces and gardens. They provide enough space for barbecue evenings with friends, relaxed sunbathing and plenty of fun in the inflatable wading pool. One of the key components is the private garden. The houses on the ground level have a 25 m² garden and a terrace of 1 m². Units on the first and second level feature a 2 m² terrace with boxes for plants. Each unit is equipped with two to three wooden flaps, which serve as a terrace when opened. When the users are not there during the week, it is possible to simply close the flaps and protect the house from unwanted peeks.

The open spaces are structured into smaller sections that can be used by the occupants. Cube-shaped seats provide an opportunity to relax and pass the time. The leisure facility offers a small coffee-to-go café with two terraces, which forms a meeting point for residents and visitors. Another important aspect is the large bike storage room where the residents can leave their bicycles. The site is located right next to a bicycle trail, and this provides an additional incentive to simply leave the car behind and make trips to the vineyards instead.

Elevation

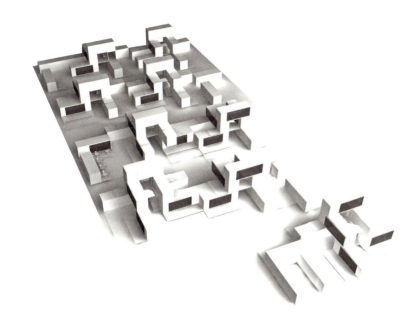

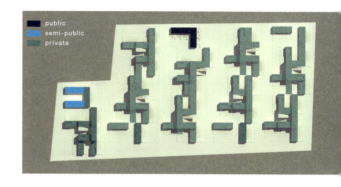

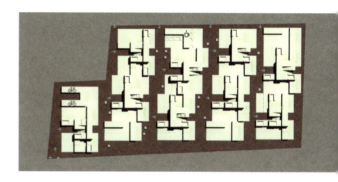

Building development

Circulation

Open space

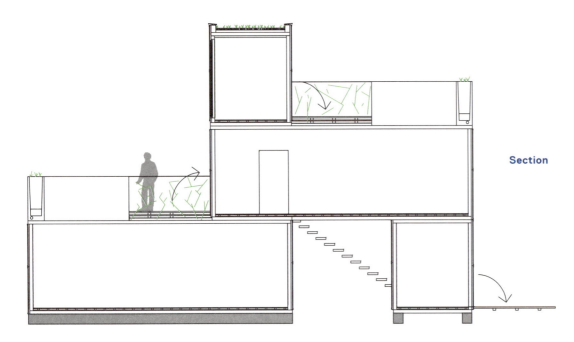

Section

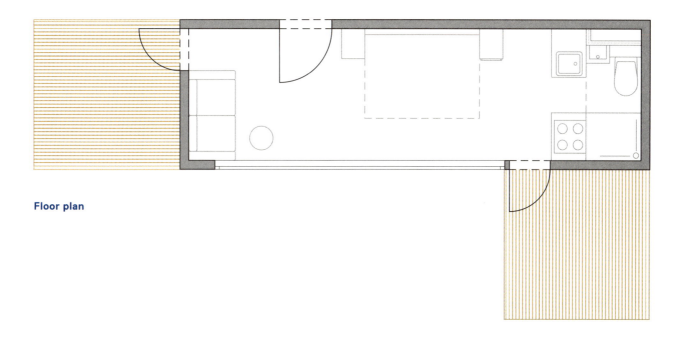

Floor plan

Multifunctional furniture

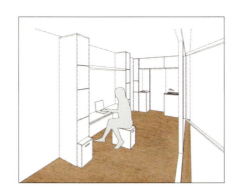
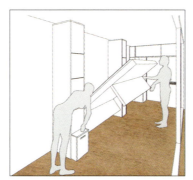

Adele J. Gindlstrasser
Instructor

RAHM architekten

Adele J. Gindlstrasser,
Ursula Musil and
Hans Schartner

Founded 2003
Based in Vienna

Row-House Estate in Eibesbrunn
Eibesbrunn, Austria, 2007
RAHM architekten, manka*musil

For the project *housing, now!* I offered my students two more parameters in addition to the institute's specifications. I first chose a real site and then gave the students the task of defining a target group for which they wanted to plan at this location. Both requirements – so I hoped – would make the task more concrete and thus allow them to regard it in a more intense, although special way.

I selected a site in a rural community in the greater Vienna area. Eibesbrunn, situated on the road leading to Brno, has a low-rise, predominantly closed development structure. Some remarkable buildings have been completed in this area in the course of the construction of Vienna's outer ring expressway and the new A5 freeway to Brno, with a substantial impact on the previous layout of the village. The suburban rail connections make the adjacent countryside, which adjoins the gently rolling hills of the Weinviertel, a potential recreational area for the city. I combined this place with an unusually high floor space ratio of 0.3. The intention was indeed to evoke a certain creative tension with the surrounding development. I was interested in the following questions: To what extent can the building task be regarded as autonomous? Is a choice of facilities necessary for the neighborhood? Is a counterpoint at all "endurable" or could it even constitute an added value for the environment?

The students' answers range from individual, autonomous high-rise buildings to extensive, terraced atrium houses, from the creation of an intercultural center to inspirations drawn from the typical rows of wine cellars or even the creation of stacked allotment garden houses as a way of deliberately negating the specifications.

My second requirement for the students was to decide for which specific group of people they wanted to realize "living" at this place. In this respect, I assumed that by concentrating on a specific target group it would be possible to analyze the group's particular lifestyle and elaborate on it, with the necessary result of having an effect on the architecture. Here I drew loose inspiration from Bernhard Rudofsky: "What we need is not a new way of building but a new way of living".

That is why the students' projects deal with issues such as "young living", with constantly changing spatial requirements; building for "young and old", which includes the realization of different requirements in a single structure; "recluse" living, with minimal spatial requirements in a dug-in style of construction; and the "collective", with minimized individual space and extensive common facilities.

Getting back to the beginning of my account, I hope – I expect – that the students will transfer the insights gained from the thorough analysis of these particular specifications to complex architectural tasks and that they will make use of the acquired experience in their future work.

House Weißgasse
Vienna, Austria, 2009

Con[Trans]
Transportable Containers

Markus Göschl
Alena Preldzic
Students

Ulrike Hausdorf
Instructor

Floor space index   0.5

Plot area   5,000 m²
Gross floor area   2,500 m²
Total usable floor space   1,838 m²

Private open space   202 m²
Public space   1,822 m²

Housing units   31

Type of construction
Prefabricated cross-laminated
wood construction

Con[Trans] – Transportable Containers

The task was to choose a 1,000 m² building site and design a construction with a variable floor space index of 0.5 – 1.0. Apart from the density, the key aspects of structure / prefabrication / type of construction were emphasized and at least one of them had to be elaborated and outlined in detail.

Location: Wachau, Lower Austria. The Wachau is a region in Lower Austria between the towns of Melk and Krems, situated approximately 80 kilometers to the west of the capital Vienna. The hillside construction site faces south and is bordered by the river Danube. The vicinity is characterized by vineyards and orchards, the surrounding villages consist of two and three-story buildings.

Minimal rooms, easy transportability, variable floor plans / positioning, open spaces, views and pre-fabrication were the most important requirements that we tried to meet in our project.

Our design was based on the maximum size of height for a truck (13.50 m x 2.55 m) to ensure the easy and uncomplicated transport. Furthermore, it should be possible to transport the modules by crane, boat or to enable delivery to any given location, be it the plot of land on a lakeside, the garden behind a house or the flat roof of a house. Prefabricating all elements from cross-laminated wood makes the transportation easier and avoids extensive works on site.

Four Modules

We offer a choice of 4 modules to cater for the different needs of the occupants and their personal circumstances.

Single / Student
usable floor space 26 m², terrace 27 m²

Couple 1
usable floor space 59 m², terrace 27 m²

Couple 2
usable floor space 58 m², terrace 11 m²

Family
usable floor space 122 m², terrace 27 m²

In order to offer flexibility and individuality within these elements as well, it is subsequently possible to complement the basic module with additional housing units or connect them with each other. The advantage of this system is that it can be realized more easily and faster than conventional types of construction.

By arranging the modules on the hillside plot, we were able to develop very open and flexible master plans – it should be possible to remove the elements at any time and every resident should have a view of the river Danube with private open space. With these priorities in mind, we arranged 31 modules of different sizes along the surface contour lines and thereby obtained a floor space index of 0.5.

In order to show how the modules can also be used on sites without a downslope, we designed a second development plan. For this purpose, several modules were mounted on rigid steel frames to create more open spaces as well as a better view.

Section

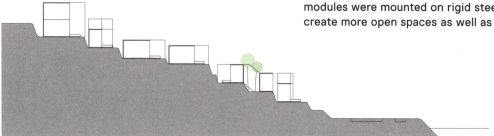

Single / Student

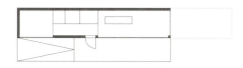 

Couple 1

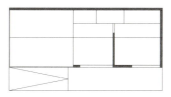 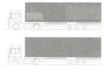

Couple 2

 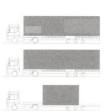

Family

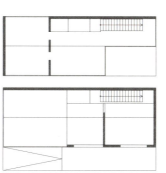 

Four modules
Floor plan and diagram

Trucks required
for transporting
the modules

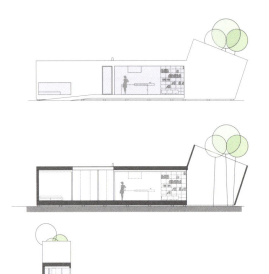

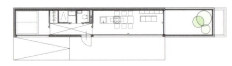

House single / student
Usable floor space 26 m²
Terrace 27 m²
GFA 34.43 m²

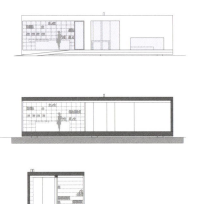

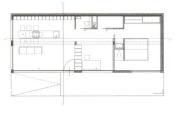

House couple 1
Usable floor space 59 m²
Terrace 27 m²
GFA 68.85 m²

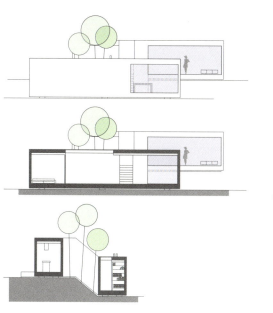

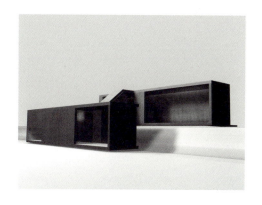

House couple 2
Usable floor space 58 m²
Terrace 11 m²
GFA 73.67 m²

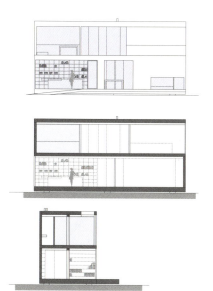

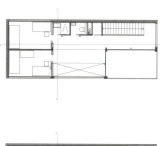

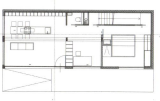

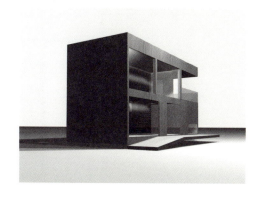

House family
Usable floor space 122 m²
Terrace 27 m²
GFA 137.70 m²

Ulrike Hausdorf
Instructor

HADLERbisHAUSDORFarchitekten

Günther Hadler and
Ulrike Hausdorf

Founded 2000
Based in Kaltenleutgeben,
Lower Austria

Housing Estate Malloth
Leopoldsdorf, Austria, 2009

**Residential Building
Eggendorfergasse**
Guntramsdorf, Austria, 2010

Breaking Through the System of Housing Construction

The majority of the population today still considers the single-family house to be ideal. Is it possible to take these wishes seriously and reconcile them with the pressure to use as little surface space as possible? Individual open space and access, privacy, far-off views?

A maximum of private open space in each unit. More space for occupants to express themselves, more space around the apartment itself – with different views of the outdoor space: these are basic needs that can be readily realized even in an apartment complex.

An ideal experimental ground for new forms of housing can be found in the dynamically evolving residential development between city and country, where conventional types of construction are no longer suitable to meet the needs of today's users. Especially in the southern area of Vienna, where migration between city and country, intensive industrial use, commercial and recreational facilities and congestion are concentrated the most, residential living requires answers to all these factors: the triad of live – work – play must be conceived and planned as a whole by application of multifunctional thinking. This was attempted already in the architecture of the seventies, for example by Harry Glück: People who flee the city want leisure facilities close by or on site. This also enables a higher development density than in the still very rural village centers or single-family house areas while minimizing leisure traffic as a side effect.

Mixed use as a fundamental condition for urbanity offers the opportunity to develop trend-setting live/work typologies instead of extensive commercial and residential areas. Such a concept would have an appropriate density of development and therefore require only little ground coverage, the proximity between the workplace and the place of residence would enable shorter travel times, reduce the dependence of workers on private transport and consequently facilitate the access to the labor market for a broader range of people from all social classes. The "work" area can comprise anything from a home office in the apartment to crafts enterprises compatible with the housing situation.

In both live-only and mixed-use spaces, the adaptability of the floor plan and room configuration is a fundamental condition for planning, all the more so as popular trends change much more quickly than the built structures.

Individual Open Space, Stacked Single-Family Houses

The "stacked single-family house" was the basic concept for a housing complex with 48 apartments in Vösendorf. All apartments are two-sided maisonettes with private open spaces (garden, loggia, balcony, terrace) and natural lighting for all rooms including bathrooms and kitchens.

A more complex variation of this principle was developed for a housing estate with 192 apartments in Leopoldsdorf near Vienna: a housing estate, situated just a few kilometers from Vienna's city limits, combining urban density on a small area, open views over the rural environment, secluded personal open spaces and leisure facilities such as a bathing pond within the complex.

Each of a range of apartment types offers different qualities: garden maisonettes, garden apartments, maisonettes extending through the depth of the building with external bathrooms. Most of the units are maisonettes, accessed by exterior corridors, interior corridors or directly from the outside. All apartments come with gardens, balconies, terraces, loggias or roof terraces.

All apartments are grouped around green courtyards opening towards the pond. The levels descending in height from south to north, the sophisticated separations and angles of the individual structures, passages and viewing openings keep the dimensions moderate and create a cozy atmosphere.

Cultural Responsibility

These days, sustainable, space-saving, landscape-friendly building is regarded as a matter of course. In residential building, planners must assume cultural responsibility for these factors as much as they need to consider the location, the housing estate and the city, something which unfortunately is still not very widespread.

The challenge now is to break through the system of housing construction, think beyond the mere minimal value and return – this also applies to the private sector – an added value to society.

Living Watzespitze

Rebecca Bremer
Nicole Neumayr
Students

Silvia Boday
Instructor

Floor space index   0.65

Plot area   5,000 m²
Gross floor area   3,250 m²
Total usable floor space   2,067 m²

Private open space   450 m²
Public space   970 m²

Housing units   15

Type of construction
Wooden framework

Living Watzespitze

The site of the project is located in Tyrol with a size of 5,000 m² and a floor space index of 0.65. The difficulty here lies in the relatively steep gradient of 10% over the entire plot, which has its highest point in the south. The task was to create homes that are adapted to the location and its inhabitants.

The basis of the concept is to model the buildings after the Tyrolean Alps, the whole design being an abstraction of these mountains. Where there is a mountain in Tyrol, there is a building on the site. Where there is a crest, there is a roof ridge. Where there is a valley, the triangular planes of the roof tilt downwards. A valley between the mountains is represented by a square on the property. The result is buildings which are very different and individual in their shape.

A building on a space of 5,000m² certainly dominates the scenery, but by breaking up the regular square pattern we managed to create a tangible expression of dominance that doesn't overawe but displays a confident quality. The regularity in the layout and the recurring theme of acute and obtuse angles convey security, but because the forms merely reappear as themes and not as concrete geometrical shapes, the senses are not offended by monotony neither in inside nor in outside spaces.

With the use of platforms of either one or two meters in height, the buildings could be successfully arranged on the 10% gradient. The difference in altitude creates protected spaces and provides each building with its own private open space. Altogether there are 16 buildings on the site, two of them two-storied, with 16 units in all.

A ramp of 6% incline offers pedestrian access. It provides a barrier-free connection to all of the units and "picks up" the occupants at their own door-step. The ramp runs through the middle of the property and, together with the buildings, surrounds the public spaces.

These paths link the public spaces and the buildings and form intimate entrances. Where the buildings converge, the paths become narrower and then open up into the public areas. The spaces are of different qualities regarding their expansion, their level and their proximity to the surrounding buildings. Car access is provided by a circular road leading to two underground parking lots. Their exits are connected with the 6% gradient pedestrian path. Two of the 16 buildings are intended for public use.

Supporting Structure

The whole supporting structure is a wood frame, a choice of material that helps the buildings blend in with the surroundings.

The construction frame consists of 30/30cm wooden members. To save costs and resources, the walls are not made of solid wood but simply clad with wood, with insulation and narrow studs at intervals of 62.5 cm on the inside.

The roof is also an abstraction of Tyrol's mountainous landscape, folding up and down along a horizontal level. We convey this idea by means of triangular roof panels, where one edge is on the highest and the other on the lowest level. In this way, the panels form ridges and valleys.

The wooden roof is sustained by beams of two different strengths. For reasons of fire safety, the beams are relatively thick and can thus be placed with a greater distance in between. The strength of the construction was also chosen due to the higher roof load requirements in Tyrol as a result of the heavy snow loads.

Access plan

Open space

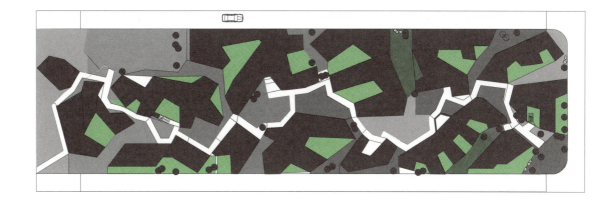

Floor plan
Ground floor

0m | 1m | 2m | 3m | 4m | 5m | 6m | 7m | 8m | 10m | 11m | 12m

64

Floor plan house 8 and 9

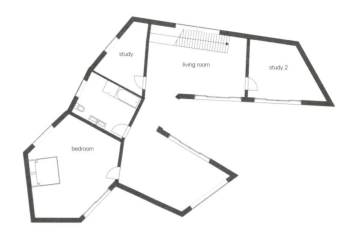

Floor plan house 6
First floor (above)
ground floor (below)

Silvia Boday
Instructor

Atelier Silvia Boday

Founded 2003
Based in Innsbruck

Three-Family House Dubis
Meran, Italy, 2007
Atelier Silvia Boday, Rainer Köberl

Three-Family House Dubis

House K in Tramin
Tramin, Italy, 2006

Housing construction must be one of the most difficult tasks and a challenge that has to be dealt with anew time and again. What, after all, is the point if not to create an optimal living space with flexible floor plans, adapted to today's needs and in constant competition with the optimal single-family house?

I am constantly trying to create space by means of simple parameters, space that makes it possible to find intimacy and experience openness at the same time. This is easier on a small scale, but it is basically always the same principle. Independently of many other influencing factors, I decided to approach the task together with the students by concentrating on two parameters that I consider to be essential: lighting and access.

The task was defined as follows: The floor space index was set to the relatively low value of 0.65; the plot is 40 m wide and 125 m long, accessible on the narrow side and ascending along its length from north to south. Last but not least, the site is located in Tyrol.

From this somewhat, let's say, unusual starting point, the students first had to deal with the question of how a building – or several buildings – must be positioned to achieve optimal lighting and orientation of the rooms. Waking up with the sun in the east, reading a book on the terrace with the setting sun in the west, and enjoying the view in the north – these ideas are associated with pleasant feelings. And isn't architecture about inspiring longing and creating atmosphere?

Based on a thorough analysis of positioning, several students succeeded in skillfully placing their structures on the plot and developing floor plans that provide for optimal natural lighting either as offset low-rise buildings or as compact single structures. At the same time, they created open spaces that permit retreat. Rail constructions with repetitive floor plans or individual solutions – everybody was able to create private open spaces.

The specified site made it possible to stack, overlap, interlink and sink the constructions into the ground. This resulted in the formation of public or semi-public spaces with different spatial qualities in between. The individual units are accessed through these areas, which also create a successful boundary to the private spaces. The access to the apartments is at least as important as the apartments themselves.

Housing always requires an individual approach; the responsibility is to create a "custom-made" space for the usually anonymous users that can be adapted to their specific needs.

Courtyard House[3]

Fabian Antosch
Mauricio Duda
Students

Feria Gharakhanzadeh
Instructor

Floor space index 1.0

Plot area   5,000 m²
Gross floor area   5,362 m²
Total usable floor space   4,021 m²

Private open space   2,283 m²
Public space   428 m²

Housing units   33

Type of construction
Solid wooden panel construction

SHOP

ATELIERS

STUDENTS

INDOOR
PLAY
GROUND

COMMON
ROOMS

BAR

ATELIERS

GALLERIES

SHOP

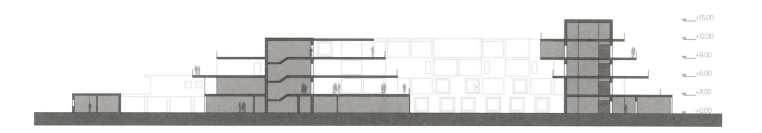

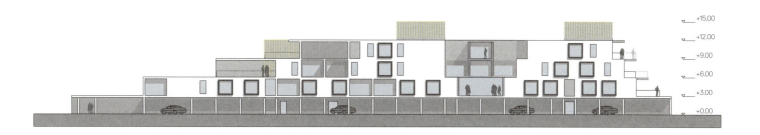

Left

Floor plan
Ground floor
First floor

Right

Section

South elevation

Courtyard House[3]

How can density in housing development be defined? The project is based on an intensive analysis dealing with modern forms of high-density development. As a consequence, we developed the following approach:

1. Own definition of density: perceived density ≠ floor space index! Constructed density generally does not correspond to apparent, perceived density.

2. Reinterpretation of predefined concepts combined with optimal application of given standards

3. Multi-dimensional layering: "... a city in which ground level zero no longer exists but has dissolved into a multiple and simultaneous presence of levels! [MVRDV]"

5. Low-rise housing development as prototype: oriental housing structures and their complex systems of spatial organization

We developed our concept according to this approach; the analysis became the basis of the scheme. The specification was a fictitious 5,000 m² construction site on the outskirts of Vienna, where a high-density low-rise housing estate with a floor space index of 1 and a special focus on prefabrication was to be constructed. The site is bordered in the north and east by multistory residential buildings and a school. A busy street is situated in the south, and an allotment garden settlement in the west.

Linking Open Space

The building with the highest possible density and the maximum permissible dimensions of the plot area of 50 x 100 m served as a starting point. That is to say, the whole construction site, i.e. the entire area of 5,000 m², is the building, and thus the density cannot be increased further. As a result,

the design was based exclusively on open space that had first been made available by means of urban development measures. Open space volume was taken from the available living space volume. The basis of the building structure is eventually defined by the development of a cross-linked (semi-) public green open space. Further development of open space on the upper levels created a network of pathways. The private open spaces were allocated as a final step in the process.

The motto is: Green space defines living space, Public space defines private space!

Development of a Residential Quarter as a High-Density Low-Rise Structure

The aim is to react to the heterogeneous environment within the building, to introduce the missing link of urban development. To connect the city limits with the beginning of the periphery, we combined different courtyard and row house types constructed next to and above each other, all consolidated in one housing complex. The variation of building types used, ranges from one-story, detached courtyard houses (next to the allotment garden settlement), to a four-story apartment house in the east with experimental housing construction on the roof.

We tried to implement all advantages of a detached single-family house and transfer them directly to a multi-story high-density courtyard house model. Consequently, every single house unit has direct neighbors and is integrated in a superordinate system. The courtyards are completely hidden from view to guarantee maximum privacy, and casual social contact is facilitated by the maximization of semi-public open space.

Type A

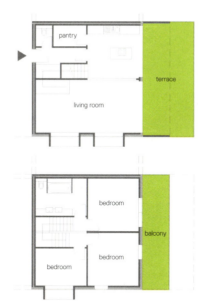

Type C

Type G

Four modules
Floor plan

Type A
inside 137 m² / outside 34 m²
Courtyard row house

Type C
inside 102 m² / outside 47 m²
Compact house

Type G
inside 152 m² / outside 91 m²
Multi-generation house

Type S
inside 83 m² / outside 16 m²
Slim house

Type S

Feria Gharakhanzadeh
Instructor

**gharakhanzadeh
sandbichler
architekten**

Feria Gharakhanzadeh and
Bruno Sandbichler

Founded 1995
Based in Vienna

House H
Vienna, Austria, 2007

Housing, Now! Density?

I want
the forest to enter my house,
the sun to shine,
the mountains to visit me.
I want to pick the fruits
of the tree through my window,
to see the driving snow, the rain, the blossoming
of the trees come and go in the mist,
the life all around grow in burgeoning vitality.
density in built-up space is quality
of life in abundance
is opening up, taking part and being able to retire
is light, air, sun, large open living space
indoors and out.

House in the Orchard, Wörgl

Prefabricated house, assembly time 1 day ... picking fruits from the children's room. A small house, made entirely of prefabricated plywood parts, stands in an orchard containing the best variety of fruits. Two cubes that, by means of their stacked arrangement, define threshold areas between inside and outside. The divisions in the glass façade, which form the structural framework, can also be used as shelves. The roof and walls of the low-energy building are made of prefabricated elements. The ground floor façade is covered by firewood stacked in the traditional manner.

House in the Orchard
Wörgl, Austria, 2004
Southern open space

Casa Nuova, Mayrhofen

Taking the large residential buildings surrounding the property as a starting point, the *Casa Nuova* housing estate represents a coherent architecture which is in keeping with today's housing comfort and which does not follow the heterogeneous canon of form of the neighboring buildings. Material and scale are oriented on regional building types, while the large windows behind horizontal bands of balconies satisfy today's matter-of-course need for enough light, air and sun.

House H, Vienna 13

The locational qualities, with garden in the north and a street in the south, give the site a sense of permeability. The building is structured by solid glass façades and is three-dimensionally subdivided with incisions in its volume. The project's exterior is characterized by a low profile and moderate proportions in relation to the environment. At the same time, the interior comes across as spacious and open, but still offering adequate intimacy.

The lower-lying floor of the living space elevates the beholder and directs the eye to the forest panorama in the north. The terrace extends the "living room/deck" into the outside. A patio is attached in the south. This open space, shielded from the street by a wall, expands the kitchen area into the outside and serves as an additional space to enjoy the sunshine – "the 5th season".

House in the Orchard
Orchard in the childrens room

Stefan Kristoffer
Susanne Mariacher
Helene Schauer
Students

Eva Česka
Instructor

Floor space index   1.1

Plot area   5,000 m²
Gross floor area   5,840 m²
Total usable floor space   3,800 m²

Private open space   1,000 m²
Public space   1,650 m²

Housing units   41

Type of construction
Panel construction

Why Does the Creation of Housing Estates so Often Lead to Spatial Monotony?

In conventional housing estates, the houses, the gardens, even entire streets are the spitting image of each other. The occupants do what they can to create a certain recognition value within their estates – they paint their houses red, blue or yellow and put up garden gnomes, wind wheels and all sorts of fences. Otherwise, finding one's way is possible only by street names and house numbers. Our project is an attempt to counteract this trend and to create a three-dimensional spatial identity.

In the course of our examination of the topic of density, we worked on a fictitious plot of land 40 x 125 m in size divided into 3 segments of different construction densities. The floor space indices are 2.5, 1.2 and 0.7, in descending order from north to south.

The experimentation with different densities and development structures directed our attention for this project to high-density low-rise construction. This led to the development of an ethereal structure of buildings, semi-public and private green spaces as well as paths and little squares.

To simplify the design, we developed 5 floor plan types, each of which are allotted one or two private open spaces in the form of courtyards, gardens or terraces. The lighting of all housing units is provided mostly by the corresponding private open spaces to ensure that the interior cannot be seen from the outside. The structure was adapted to the respective location in an optimal way by rotating, mirroring and offsetting openings and open spaces. The remainder of the plot was filled with semi-public areas that serve as access and common open space at the same time.

The result was a landscape consisting of structures whose horizontal and vertical density decreases smoothly from north to south and which makes the limits between the construction densities seem to disappear.

Floor plan

Ground floor
First floor
Second floor
Third floor

common area

private open space

housing units
a, b, c, d

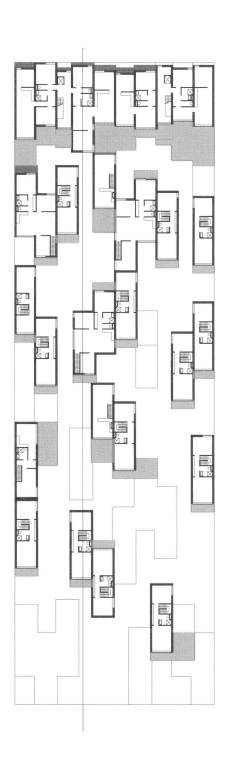
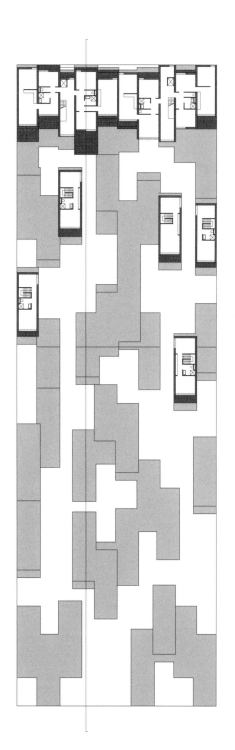

83

Section

Eva Češka
Instructor

češka priesner partner architektur

Eva Češka,
Friedrich Priesner and
Georg Hurka

Founded 1989
Based in Vienna

Housing Estate Siegergasse
Vienna, Austria, 2000

CPPA Housing Construction

In contrast to current architectural trends, our focus is on permanence. Special buildings originate from a sensitive consideration of location, client and user on the basis of an approach to architecture that is years in the making.

Personal Style Rooted in classical modernism and functionalism, the integration of subjective elements results in a personal yet functional style. The personal mark of the architects tells the story of the individual tasks.

Functionality Buildings serve a purpose. We fully support this self-evident postulate and reject any deviation which favors formalistic solutions. Subjective elements enhance the functional solution without undermining it.

Economy Building is expensive. Only a negligible minority of clients is not subject to economic constraints. Additional architectural value therefore requires careful consideration of costs and benefits. There is a life after building – and economic resources should be saved for this time.

Responding to the Location The site and its specific conditions are taken into account. The concept is created not only based on its inner logic but also considers its role in the „partnership" of the buildings, the landscape and the surroundings.

Representation of the client or user Architecture should interpret and promote the personality of the user. In housing construction, this can only mean offering a wide range of choices and enabling personal development.

Structure The logic of the inner design layout is a technical, economic and aesthetic challenge. Self-explanatory and elegant solutions are our goal.

Timelessness Our solutions are not examples of a certain year; rather, they should remain valid in the long term. We do not indicate a date of origin for our projects.

Ecology The conservation of the natural environment is a general obligation. Minimizing energy and natural resource use is fully in line with economic considerations and the permanence of the design.

Residential Building Welingergasse
Vienna, Austria, 2008

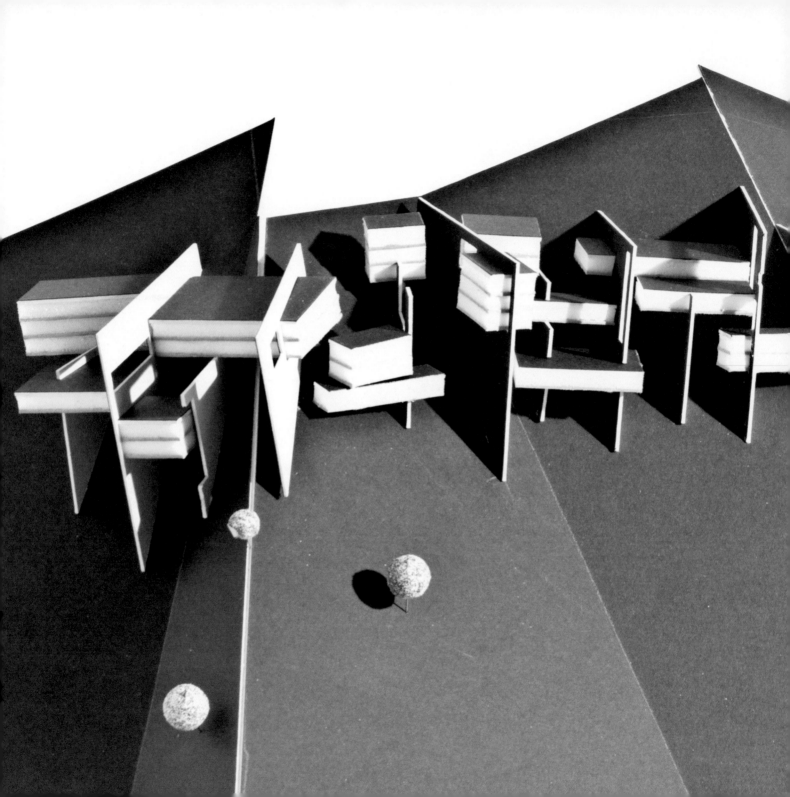

Frame Story

Emanuel Bührle
Melanie Hosner
Marius Nechville
Students

Martina Schöberl
Instructor

Floor space index   1.35

Plot area   5,900 m²
Gross floor area   7,995 m²
Total usable floor space   1,343 m²

Private open space   5,996 m²
Public space   4,797 m²

Housing units   72

Type of construction
Cross-wall construction,
reinforced concrete

Frame Story

Frame story is a housing construction project at Lake Constance in Vorarlberg which was designed on a 5,900 m² plot of land.

The name refers on the one hand to the formal components of the building, which unfolds along the hillside with a view of the lake. The main load-bearing elements of the housing estate are one-and-a-half meter thick accessible concrete slabs, force-locked with the ground by means of reinforced cast-in-place concrete poles and containing the 17 housing cubes in the form of a broken-up cross-wall construction. This construction method creates open cuboids which in these surroundings awake associations with a framed painting and inspire the imagination of the beholder.

On the other hand the name deliberately echoes the literary narrative. Offered is a scope of clearly defined character and obvious possibilities (the frame) within which the user can act and create freely (the story).

The liberties and possibilities of the residents include a spacious private garden on each roof (obtained by means of intensive planting of the entire exposed roof surface), which can be built-up and designed according to personal preferences and must only be shared with a small number of residents. An additional comfort is provided by the spacious interior design of each cube, for example by means of optional flexible partition walls. The estate is made even more user-friendly through several common rooms (sauna, swimming pool, etc.), a large, easy-to-reach underground garage, spectacular panorama elevators and a positive natural environment with impressive views of the green hillside along Lake Constance.

The capacity of the complex comprises 17 individually designed cubes with one to a maximum of three stories and an average of five multilaterally transparent housing units. The entire building is oriented to the south-west and the wide openings in the aforementioned concrete slabs provide an excellent lighting throughout.

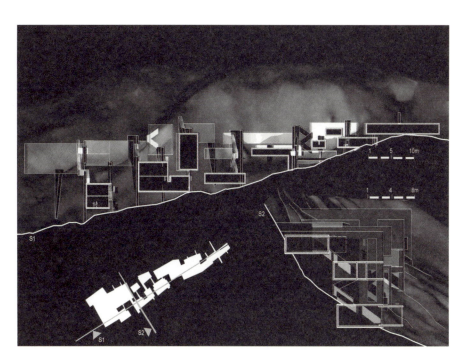

Design approach

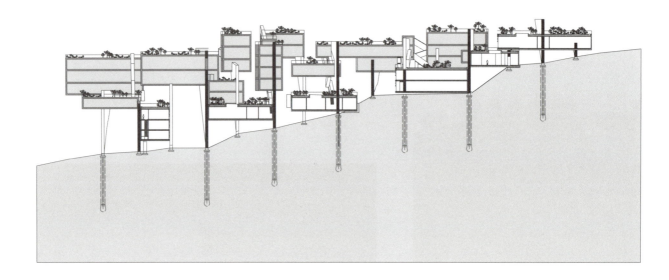

Longitudinal section

Floor plan

Right

Cross section

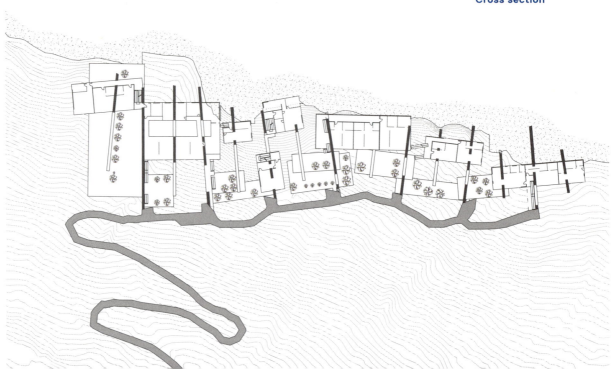

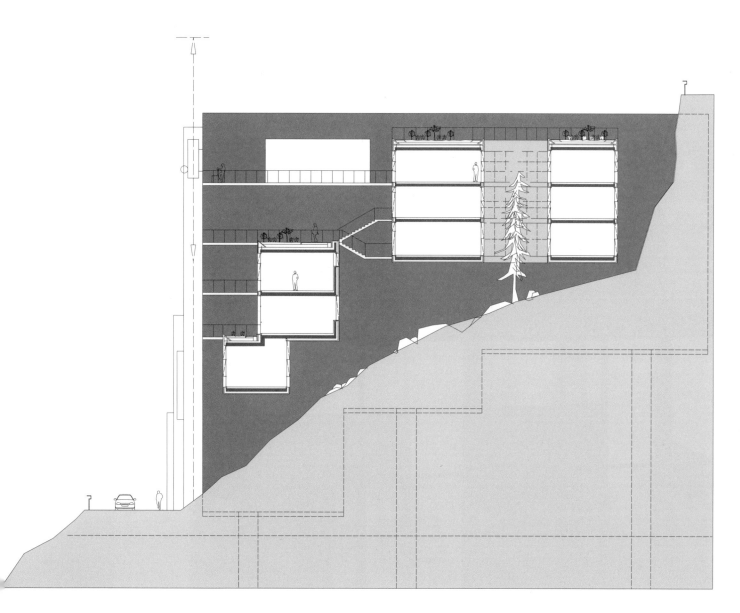

Martina Schöberl
Instructor

RATAPLAN

Rudolf Fritz,
Susanne Höhndorf,
Gerhard Huber,
Friedel Winkler and
Martina Schöberl

Founded 1993
Based in Vienna

Housing Estate Autofabrikstraße
Vienna, Austria, 1999

Some thoughts on the course and the topic of housing in general.

The Design Process as Cooperation

Instead of leading a competition of ideas, the focus in the design process was on cooperation. A team that works well together can compile experience and knowledge to form a multifaceted overall concept. The beginning of the process, in which the intended result is formulated, is especially important. The foundations for all further work are laid in this initial stage, which also forms the basis for flexibility in all subsequent steps.

Each team puts its approach and concepts forward for discussion, not only to review its own work but also to convey the ideas and analyze them. Different views are argued in the team and compromises have to be found together. The hierarchy among the decision-makers is replaced by qualitative decisions, responsiveness to arguments and discussing of objective reasons. Everyone acts within the scope of the common concept. This approach means letting the ideas grow instead of just forcing them through.

Orientation in the Process

The experience gained in the development of groundwork can be communicated only in part. In the course of approaching the subject, a process of personal development takes place. It is the complexity and depth that with time grow for each and every one, both as an individual and as a group. It simply is not possible to express specifications appropriate for design in terms of numbers, norms or a fixed framework because requirements which take the form of norms can only describe a certain standard. Architectural quality as a response to needs requires an intense examination of the subject. In doing so, it is especially important not to permit the initial idea to become watered down and to make sure that the concrete utopian vision is not lost.

The Residents' Everyday Reality

It would be a much too narrow view of things to plan for a particular individual in a certain phase of life from the beginning; people's living conditions and needs change over time. For the majority of residential buildings and in social housing, the residents are not known in the early planning stage, but this clientele usually has one thing in common: father, mother, 1-2 children. This can lead to the development of "ghettos" for small families and, as one in three marriages is divorced, to serious housing problems after a divorce.

Therefore, it is essential to offer solutions that correspond to the everyday reality and which take into account the need for flexibility in the subsequent phases of life. The most important prerequisite that allows people to adopt public spaces is probably the identification with the place, something that reflects their own personal reality and enables them to establish a connection.

The development of a central theme, an ideal or even a utopian vision could help create a new type of approach: an overall concept that is farther-reaching, intellectually less restricted, more courageous and freer than that what can possibly be realized in a certain era.

Mansion Houses
Maurer Stadtvillen
Vienna, Austria, 2005

The Inner World of the Outside World of the Inner World

Eva Liisa Freuis-Manhart
Student

Franziska Orso
Instructor

Floor space index   1.4

Plot area   5,000 m²
Gross floor area   7,234 m²
Total usable floor space   6,498 m²

Private open space   1,521 m²
Public space   3,729 m²

Housing units   56

Type of construction
Reinforced concrete, wooden
frame construction

The Inner World of the Outside World of the Inner World – Courtyard Houses

The specifications for our group under the guidance of Franziska Orso were a floor space index of 1.5 and a plot size of 50 x 100 meter.

No particular construction site was determined, only that the structure had to be based on the style of the single-family house estates in the 22nd district of Vienna. This enabled a prototypical approach to the task. The aim was to develop a new structure integrating the positive aspects of these structures, such as privacy and open space, in the design. In spite of the size of the plot, I tried to incorporate the subject of the courtyard house in my design and to find a solution for the access of the building.

The courtyard house offers a high living quality by means of a clearly delimited private open space. The outside is brought to the interior as a piece of transmuted nature that is restored within the protecting walls of the architecture. It features an inner courtyard enclosed from all sides that serves as an orientation for the surrounding rooms. The courtyard structure provides a better protection of privacy through the (windowless) separating wall, while the garden is consolidated in a compact form. The size of the plot can be considerably smaller.

The houses are accessed through individual staircases with glass walls on the ground floor, which promotes social contact and communication by means of ample open space including parking spaces. The ground floor area should offer the possibility to repair one's bicycle, wash one's car, meet one's neighbors or just socialize. Lighting is provided by a glass façade around the ground floor (noise protection) and openings through which trees grow into the courtyards of the houses on the upper floor. The occupants are invited to choose their courtyard house not only based on two different sizes, but also by considering the different types of trees requiring different care. According to Vienna's Department of Parks and Gardens, the following species of trees would be suitable to grow under these conditions: columnar hornbeam, cypress oak, columnar maple, elm, tree of heaven, purple leaf plum and Japanese cherry, of which the native species are more appropriate because they cope better with dry conditions.

Construction The supports on the ground floor and the ceiling slab to the upper floor are made of reinforced concrete, the walls on the first and second floor are a wood frame construction clad with wooden shingles and the roof elements are prefabricated of laminated wood.

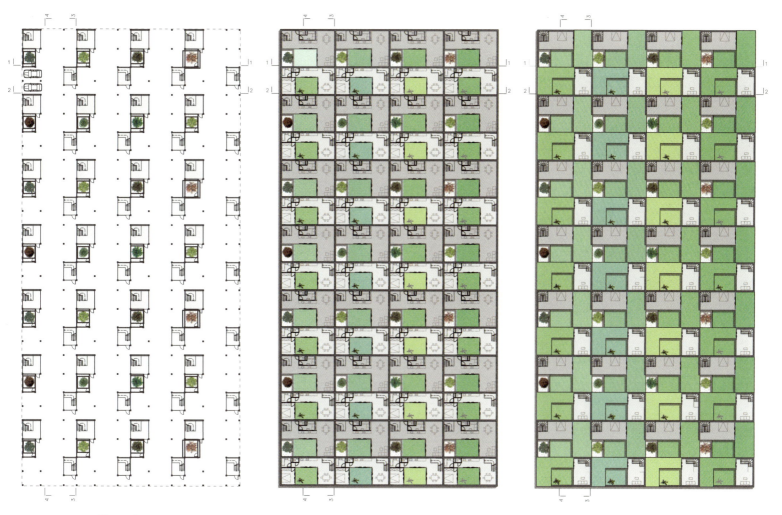

Floor plan

Ground floor
First floor
Second floor

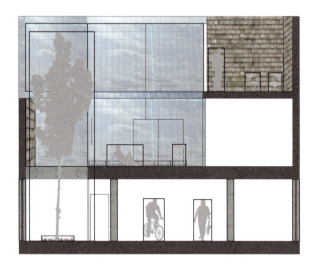

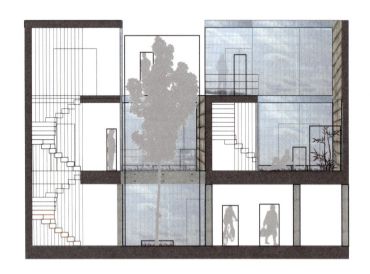

Sections

Above: 1-1
Below: 2-2

Right

Floor plan

Ground floor
First floor
Second floor
Roof plan

Entrance Hall

Courtyard

WC

Bath

Living Room

Courtyard

Bath

WC

Kitchen/Dining

Courtyard

Bedroom

Entrance Hall

Bedroom

Terrace

Living Room

Franziska Orso
Instructor

orso.pitro

Franziska Orso and
Ulrike Pitro

Founded 2007
Based in Vienna

**R.D.P. Settlement in Mpumalanga
South Africa, 2001**

Two examples of cul-de-sacs

Above: developed without
adapting to existing structures.
Below: developed around
an existing old-core house.

Housing as a Basis

Housing can never be regarded on its own; it must always be seen in context. Even if we consider the function of housing in the narrower sense as a series of activities of private housekeeping, these activities begin and end outside of the private living space. The home is the spatial center in our lives; as such, it forms part of a spatial arrangement of functions and interacts with its specific environment.

The aim is to create a basis for the development of living space which enables the residents to express themselves without temporal restrictions. Especially in the production of living space for the masses, where the project is usually determined by funding systems, a tight corset of rules and specifications often exists that does not leave much room for development potential. Here it would suffice to keep the framework just slightly more flexible in order to allow a housing system to function.

I would like to illustrate this with an example from South Africa and show how the functionality of a project can be influenced by the combination of context and specifications that still leave scope for development. Perhaps it is possible to discover a new perception of one's own situation by stepping out of the familiar environment and analyzing other processes of living space creation.

After the end of Apartheid in 1994, the government of South Africa initiated a development plan that included promoting the construction of low-cost housing as a way of coming to grips with the housing shortage in the country. The government-funded sites are 250 m² developed plots of land with a 30 m² one-room house that can subsequently be enlarged by their occupants. Mono-functional mass housing settlements with rows of uniform houses are emerging in the sprawling periphery of the city, far from offering any possibility for development. Due to the location on the margins of the city and the lack of any urban functions, these areas are unable to develop economically or socially.

In terms of its fundamental structure, Alexandra, a small township near Johannesburg that was originally planned as housing-only, does not differ much from such settlements. The basic conditions which led to Alexandra's favorable development are unusual for black townships. It is the only black township in Johannesburg that is integrated into the city structure and, moreover, the government allowed the black population there to own land even during Apartheid. Owing to its proximity to employment opportunities, Alexandra was and is an important transit point for newcomers seeking work in Johannesburg.

The basic structure is formed by a rigid orthogonal grid of streets with houses that were erected between 1920 and the Second World War. Over the years, these so-called old core houses were repeatedly adapted and enlarged by their occupants, and the originally 1,200 m² plots of land were divided into smaller parcels. This led to the development of a new access system consisting of secondary cul-de-sacs. The cul-de-sacs have a courtyard-like quality, somewhere between private and public, a secluded space for smaller communities in close proximity to the busy main roads. Today, Alexandra covers an area of 460 ha and has a population of 350,000 people.

Starting from a loose basic structure that offered enough scope in spite of its rigidity, Alexandra over time developed into a unique social and urban structure and could be regarded in many ways as a model for future strategies of urban development projects in South Africa.

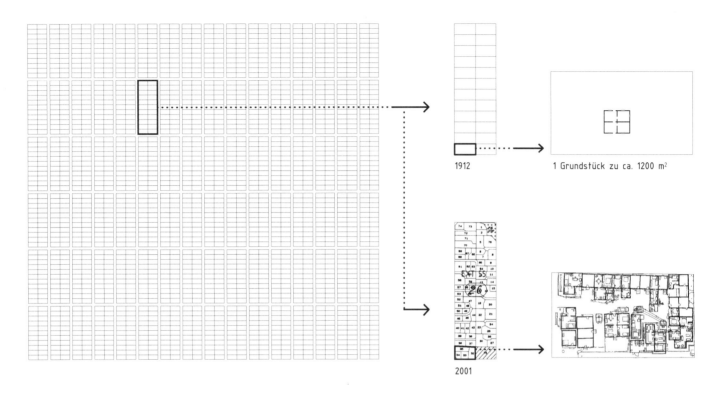

1912

1 Grundstück zu ca. 1200 m²

2001

Development of the
basic structure of
Alexandra Township
from 1912 to 2001

Detail of the settlement
structure of Alexandra
Township, 2001

45.425277° / 12.327219°

Johannes Ritsch
Sarah Wantoch
Students

Kinayeh Geiswinkler-Aziz
Instructor

Floor space index   1.65

Plot area   2,300 m²
Gross floor area   3,814 m²
Total usable floor space   1,827 m²

Private open space   364 m²
Public space   495 m²

Housing units   30

Type of construction
Reinforced concrete

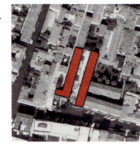

1.

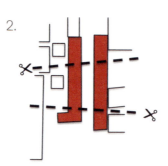

2.

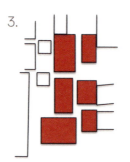

3.

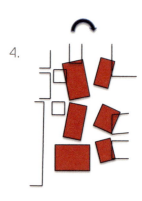

4.

Urban development

Section

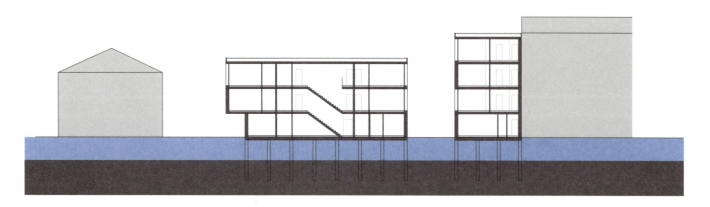

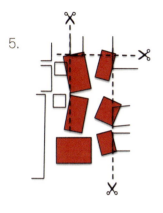

5.

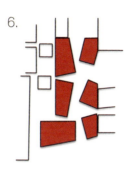

6.

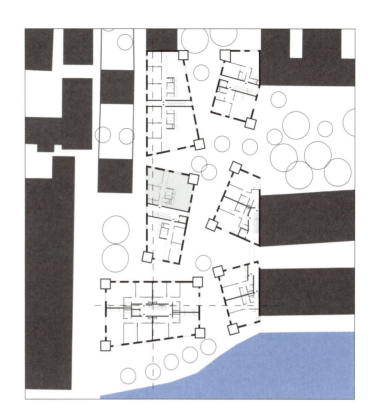

Floor plans

First floor
Ground floor

shops / offices

common area

restaurant

playroom for children

Our aim was to use the new structures to break up the existing development of the plot and thus create an interesting spatial setting. This was achieved in several steps:

Existing development
Breaking-up of the existing development
Creation of new orthogonal structures
Rotation of the buildings
Adaptation to the surroundings
New structures

Rotating the buildings formed some intriguing "in-between" spaces whose many differences spark an interest to explore them. The construction resulted in narrow passages and small squares where the residents can spend their time.

Special attention was also paid to the adjoining properties. The parks and green areas are provided with the necessary space to extend into the newly built-up site. Paths are continued. On the side facing the canal, an open space was created right by the water as an inviting place for residents to pass the time. The two- to four-story buildings are integrated into their respective surroundings.

In addition to the urban development approach, we took visual relations as a starting point for our design. The goal was to offer the residents different and intriguing views. In some parts, it is possible to overlook the other buildings, in others to look between them. Unexpected views entice passers-by to explore around the next corner – as is often the case in Venice. The use of the ground floor ranges from public to private. There are shops and offices, playrooms for small children, common rooms and storage rooms. The apartments on the upper floors all come with a private terrace.

We focused on the creation of sustainable floor plans with easy adaptation to use. The façade reflects the small-scale character of the city – varied and diverse and, thanks to the external shutters, variable.

Detailed façade section

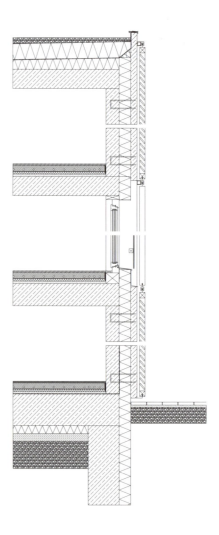

Detailed floor plan

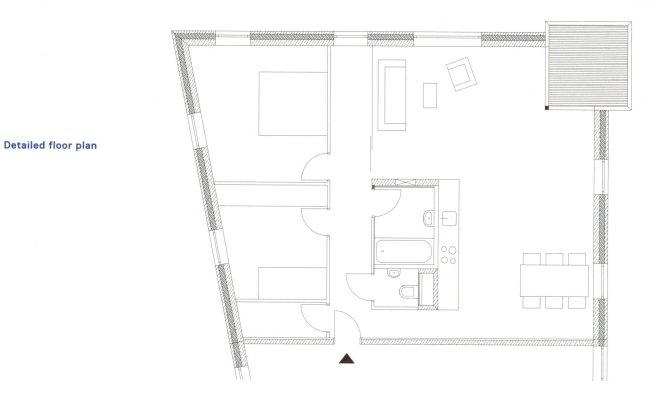

Kinayeh Geiswinkler-Aziz
Instructor

**Geiswinkler & Geiswinkler –
Architekten ZT GmbH**

Kinayeh Geiswinkler-Aziz and
Markus Geiswinkler

Founded 1990
Based in Vienna

Karree St. Marx
Vienna, Austria, 2009

Left

Garden Estate Am Hofgartel
Vienna, Austria, 2003

Vertical Garden House
Alxingergasse
Vienna, Austria, 2005

Housing Construction – in Principle

After a long absence in the public dialogue, the topic of housing construction has recently been picked up again by the architectural discourse – and with good reason. Housing is one of the most elemental issues of architecture; everybody is involved; everybody has his or her own experiences and opinions; as a result, no architectural subject can be discussed with the general public in the same way. The development of housing is determined by the interaction between possibilities and rules, between challenge and self-restraint. First and foremost, housing must meet the needs of the user – the utility and not the spectacle is at the fore. Housing is characterized by its location and influences the location in turn.

Housing and Urban Development

Housing is the elemental component of the city. The character of a city is formed by its basic element-housing. Urban development presupposes housing – but housing can exist without urban development. The foundation stone of housing is the instrumental element in urban development. The location in the city influences the structure of the housing. It constitutes the urban spaces – defines the framework in which the special elements of the city are integrated. The urban spaces form the character of a city – and the basic elements must adapt to this genius loci accordingly; each new housing task is a part of the big picture.

Housing and Open Space

Housing engages in a dialog with its environment. This makes the surrounding open space of vital importance. An essential prerequisite is to have a clear hierarchy of open spaces: the public open space is juxtaposed against the residential (common or private) open space. The design of the open spaces is defined by the degree of publicness or privacy. Different threshold areas form transitions between the open spaces and the living space. The relation of privacy and publicness of the open spaces is determined by the character of the city and the location of the building within the city.

The Residential Building

The residential building provides space for different necessities of life. The socio-political development of a city is reflected in these needs. An open, heterogeneous society requires differentiated, adaptable (living) space. The residential building and its facilities must therefore react with the appropriate flexibility to those changing needs. The issue here is not to set up a neutral framework as a standard, but the ability to change and adapt to the requirements over time. The dynamic of changeability of a residential building depends on its location in the urban setting.

Conclusion

Housing directly influences the living conditions of the people. The development of quality housing must therefore be based on responsibility and reason.

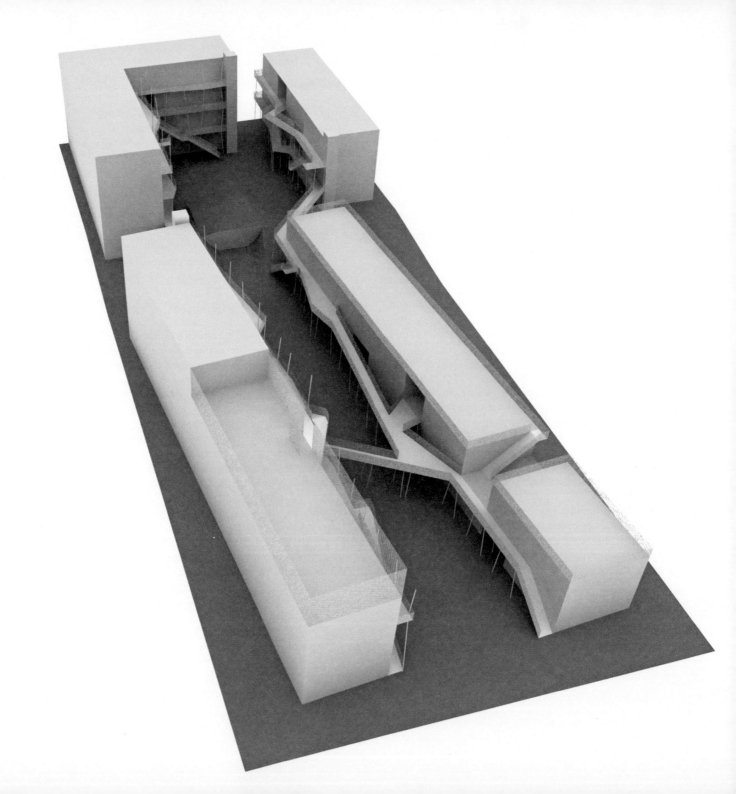

Green Modules

Viktoria Jiru
Christian Daschek
Students

Marlies Breuss
Instructor

Floor space index   1.7

Plot area   5,000 m²
Gross floor area   8,675 m²
Total usable floor space   2,880 m²

Private open space   1,500 m²
Public space   3,562 m²

Housing units   48

Type of construction
Wooden panel construction

Design approach

Left: Users : entire lifespan
Right: Concept flexible
living space

1	single
2	couple
3	family
4	retiree

1	single
2	couple
3	family
4	retiree
5	two singles

1 open living and working space

2 separate rooms, more dedicated living space

3 separate rooms, more dedicated living space, additional private rooms necessary

4 open living space, more dedicated living space

5 separate rooms and working space, additional private rooms necessary

Concept apartment prototypes

Right: scheme A with sliding walls
Below: scheme B with movable
furniture elements

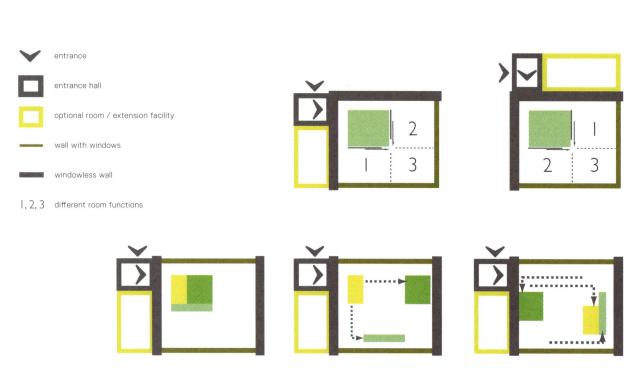

entrance

entrance hall

optional room / extension facility

wall with windows

windowless wall

1, 2, 3   different room functions

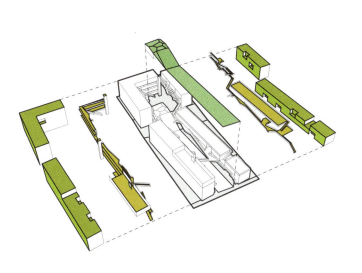

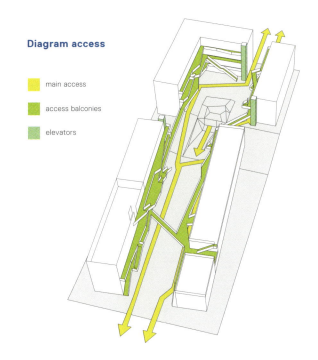

Diagram access

▮ main access

▮ access balconies

▮ elevators

Plan of the housing complex

General characteristics:
Compact longitudinal residential
blocks frame the area.
Public green open space for the
residents in the center.
Exterior corridors with spaces in
between form a semi-public zone.

Diagram open space

▮ public green space

▮ playground

▮ semi-private area / wooden terrace

▮ exterior corridor

▮ solar power generation

▮ herb and vegtable garden

▮ roof garden

▮ private garden

▮ waste collection area

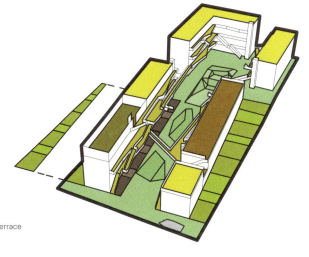

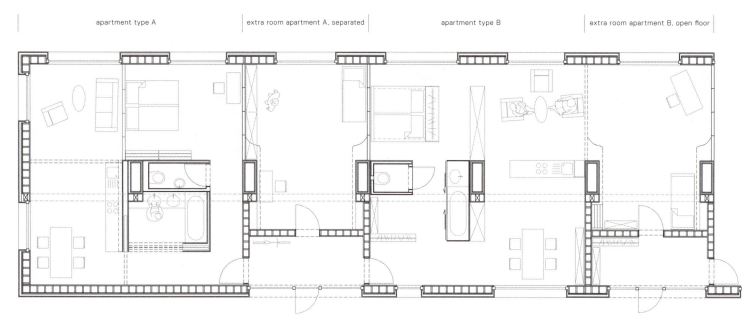

| apartment type A | extra room apartment A, separated | apartment type B | extra room apartment B, open floor |

Floor plan
Sample use

Green Modules

The starting point for our housing project was an analysis of housing space usage of different people in different social situations. In the course of a lifetime, however, user profiles and, consequently, user-needs change. That is why we were searching for a solution that caters for the different requirements in a flexible way.

Based on this concept, we developed two apartment prototypes that allow for a flexible room layout by means of displaceable dividing walls and mobile room elements. Additionally, each prototype has adjoining rooms that can be either attached to the apartment or accessed and used separately. In this way, it is possible to meet different space requirements. In the event that the optional room is not used, it can be rented to third parties or used as a common area in the residential building.

The project is situated on a longitudinally extended plot of land between two roads. For this reason, the two main entrances are located on the main access points in the east and west. The orientation of the residential block is aligned with the surrounding buildings.

The housing complex comprises 24 housing units and 36 connectable rooms per prototype and is structured into three elements: an open green space with a multipurpose hall is framed by compact longitudinal residential blocks; in between, there is a semi-private transitional zone with exterior corridors broadening and narrowing at different angles.

The residential building itself is made up of a system of prefabricated wooden panel units. The actual load-bearing structure consists of the wooden panels, secured against buckling by wooden supports from behind. Only one additional girder per apartment is necessary. Every residential block is built to the passive house standard with controlled ventilation.

The system of exterior corridors is a free-standing, wood-paneled steel structure of individually prefabricated elements, attached to the façade only by means of a few safety anchors. The corridors are sustained by thin, angular supports. Their walls are covered with vegetation and they form a boundary to the neighboring open space. On the north side, they are semi-detached from the façade to enable daylight illumination; on the south side, they line the façade directly to provide shade. The roof areas can be used as additional green space or for solar panels.

The ground floor features business premises available for renting and common rooms such as laundry facilities and a recreation area. The multipurpose hall can be accessed directly from the open space. The open spaces comprise green space and recreational space, a vegetable garden, green areas with terraces on the roof as well as two playgrounds.

Marlies Breuss
Instructor

HOLODECK architects

Marlies Breuss and
Michael Ogertschnig

Founded 1998
Based in Vienna

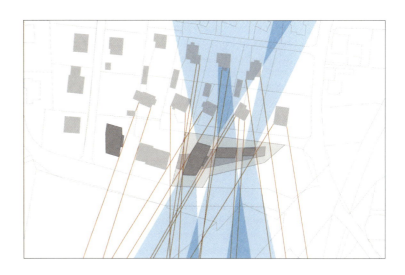

22 Tops
Wolfsberg, Austria, 2008

Housing, Now!

In our view, designing densified housing structures is one of the most complex project tasks in architecture. On the one hand, the concept design will have to be based on maximum flexibility that will allow for affordable units and cater to as diverse a group of users as possible; on the other hand, each room becomes a highly personal long-term living space for the occupants. Anonymity and familiarity, privacy and public life, multitude and singularity, individual and community – these are just some of the dichotomies we consider to reinterpret densified housing buildings by means of analytical results.

In the housing, now! design studio, we focus especially on the investigation of possible future housing types applying criteria such as 'flexibility, extensibility, open space' and, concerning the subject of construction in particular, on the pre-fabrication of building elements, whereas the level of prefabrication in the end is defined by the design.

The individual housing typologies are developed in several working phases. The first stage includes a thorough analysis of the daily functional routines in the housing unit and of the amount of time the different users spend there in their everyday lives (single persons, DINKs, families, senior citizens) during the week. The observation of the inhabitant's behavioral patterns facilitates an optimization of space and, further on, new spatial combinations are defined for improved living spaces. With the so-called 'prototype models', the insights thus obtained are transformed into new housing concepts.

The second phase focuses on the task of prefabrication combined with the highest possible flexibility. The use of prefabricated elements must not reduce the flexibility of the housing concept achieved in the 'prototype model', but should help realize the building construction in an optimized way. The development of 'structural models' makes it possible to frequently reconsider the decisions made on prefabrication and to observe the inherent consequences on the intertwined structure.

The integration of the 'structural model' into the contextual fabric of the surrounding environment is examined in the final phase. Scale, orientation, light, local building regulations such as density, power generation, a maximum variety of common rooms and different available open spaces influence the 'structural model' and give the project its specific local character.

The relative density of the housing projects is not specified at the start of this studio; rather, it is determined on the basis of each housing concept prototype with a special focus on the selected site and its environmental requirements. An inversion of the actual design process (in which the density determines the compactness of the structure from the beginning) enables other perspectives and design strategies, a process that is part of our office's design strategy.

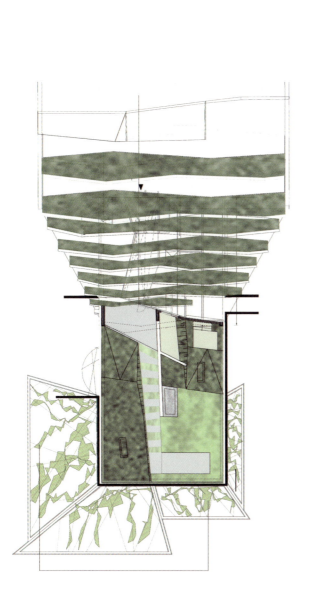

Stratified Townscape
Vienna, Austria, 2008
Concept 'greenliving'

Green Crossover

Michael Strodl
Maximilian Bauböck
Students

Ursula Schneider
Instructor

Floor space index   2.5

Plot area   5,000 m²
Gross floor area   12,700 m²
Total usable floor space   7,400 m²

Private open space   3,600 m²
Public space   950 m²

Housing units   80

Type of construction
Reinforced concrete

Green Crossover

The starting point for our design exercise was a site of our choosing measuring 5,000 m² to be developed with a floor space index of 2.5. Special criteria included open space (public/private), green zones (roof/façade), mixed use (living/working), lighting and shading (winter/summer).

The project is located on a fictitious plot of land in the suburbs of Vienna. An ample green belt is situated in the north-east – the south-east is dominated by an urban environment. Our aim was to create a connection between the two existing zones. This is reflected by the large ramps that form a link between the two areas through an inner courtyard. We tried to incorporate both nature and aspects of urban life in our concept.

The aspect of nature shows in our façade design as well as the spacious roof terraces with vegetation. The façade is fitted with soil-filled boxes for plants. The boxes line the entire building façade and are designed to enhance the microclimate, improve the air quality and have a positive effect on the appearance of the building. The roof terraces with vegetation are situated on different floors of the building and provide public as well as private open space with zones that can be utilized individually. The additional thermal insulation effect of the green roof also helps save energy.

The aspect of urban life shows itself in the ground floor area, which offers space for shops and retail premises, and in the transition between city and nature by means of an inner courtyard with café.

The building is composed of two connected parts. The first, a compact structure with interior hallway access that opens up to the east on the upper floors, forms a gallery that provides natural lighting on all levels including the ground floor. The second structure is divided into two legs extending to the south-east. The interjacent space features public as well as private open space, separated by the access passage.

There are four categories of apartments available, ranging from smaller two-room apartments to two-floor maisonettes with private roof terraces. One of the essential design features are the loggias, formed by offsetting the openings to the interior of the building. In this way, each apartment is allotted additional open space.

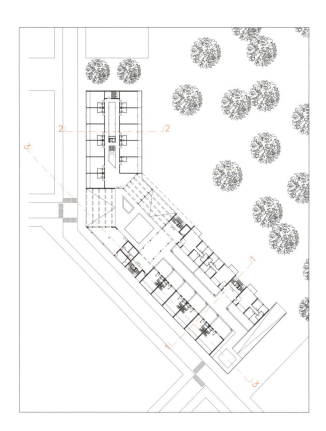

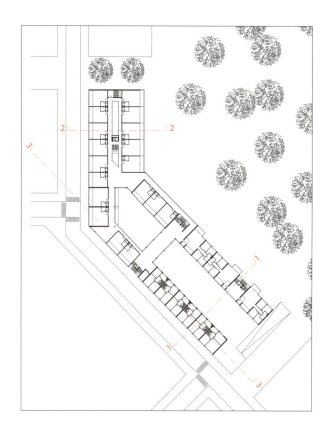

Floor plan
Ground floor
First floor

Site plan

Solar evaluation
Winter sun, ca 20°

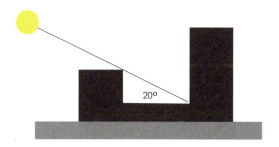

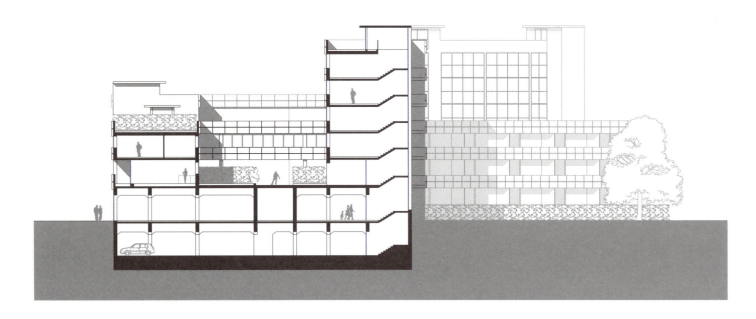

Section 1-1

Maisonette

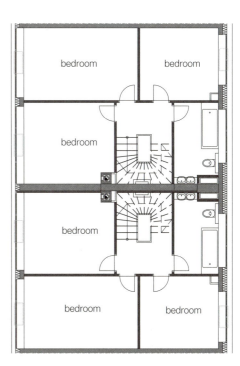

Detailed section

Vertical greening
Soil-filled zinc sheet metal containers

Horizontal greening
20 cm vegetation layer
Filter layer
8 cm drainage gravel
Separating layer
30 cm insulation XPS
Separating layer
Multi-layered moisture-proof PE
6 cm sloping screed
22 cm reinforced concrete

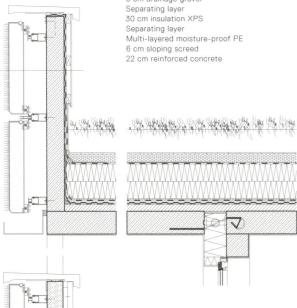

Ursula Schneider
Instructor

pos sustainable architecture

Ursula Schneider,
Fritz Oettl and
Claire Poutaraud

Founded 2000
Based in Vienna

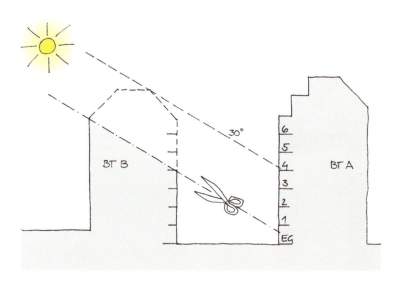

Passive House Estate Eurogate
Competition, preliminary design
Vienna, Austria, 2007

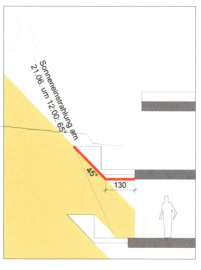

Sonneneinstrahlung am 21.06. um 12:00: 65°

45°

130

SUN Power City
Concept and test design for an
energy-generating city district
Vienna, Austria
Start of planning 2008

Density and Sustainable Housing Construction

The question of density plays an important role in several aspects of sustainable building. In general, a medium to higher density is regarded as a basic prerequisite for energy efficiency in a building. Smaller-volume single-family houses or row houses have a higher surface-area-to-volume ratio, which must be compensated with sometimes considerably higher strengths of insulating material if similar results in energy consumption as with compact larger-volume buildings are desired. Furthermore, a lower density takes up more land and thus adds to urban sprawl.

This also has substantial secondary consequences for energy use – in regions of low density, it is not economically feasible to offer public transport or district heating, develop renewable energy networks such as geothermal power or provide a social infrastructure that is within walking distance or accessible by bicycle.

If our aim is to achieve a carbon-neutral building sector and to focus on the building envelope as a source of power generation, the density is currently limited by the proportion of the power output that can be obtained through photovoltaic modules on the structure to the energy use of the respective building. Given minimal energy use, adaptation of the urban development design and the optimal use of photovoltaics in the building, 100% coverage is already possible in Central Europe for floor space indices up to 2.0 in the annual average (with grid feed-in); given less optimal conditions, 100% coverage rates with photovoltaic electricity currently lie more within the range of a floor space index of 1 and below. The amount of light and sun in a building are two additional quality criteria in housing construction that are strongly influenced by density.

We believe that 30° or higher shading from surrounding buildings (not the 45° permissible in the building regulations, rotated laterally) is not appropriate for sustainable housing construction and that the windows should cover a minimum of 25% of the usable space behind them. We clearly favor orienting the building to the south or SSW/SSE to make use of the sunlight because it can provide the interior with abundant direct sunlight when the sun is low in winter and can be easily shaded with a simple projecting roof in summer. The east-west orientation is in our judgment not suitable to provide the building with enough sunlight in winter. Moreover, the passive solar yield of a south-facing building has a clear positive effect on the energy balance, although we find the proven favorable physiological effects on the human organism to be even more important (prevents winter depression).

A higher density usually also leads to an increase in the chosen tract depths. This in turn has consequences for the ratio of façade surface to usable floor space. Considering the real take-home pay since 1995, a priority in housing construction must be to offer good, spacious floor plans on a small space with an additional option for several individual rooms. There is a high demand for single parent apartments with 60 m² and 3 rooms. Such floor plans can only be provided if enough façade length is available. The previously described interrelations serve us as a basis for decision-making in the planning of housing construction.

The aim of our work is to provide apartments that are bright, have enough sunlight in winter, offer controllable thermal conditions in summer and possess private open space of sufficient size without blocking light to the apartments below, apartments that consume a minimum of primary energy over their entire lifespan, offer the possibility to use the building envelope for power generation in the future, have a high indoor air quality thanks to the material chosen and convey a more spacious image in relation to their floor space.

Housing Square

Bernd Hattinger
Fabian Lutter
Students

Susanne Fritzer
Instructor

Floor space index   2.5

Plot area   5,000 m²
Gross floor area   12,687 m² (total)
Total usable floor space   11,175 m²

Private open space   2,175 m²
Public space   4,739 m²

Housing units   96

Type of construction
Concrete frame with structural core

Housing Square

The subject of the studio was to examine the concept of density in architecture. The initial situation was marked by the selection of an appropriate location for the designated 5,000 m² site. Our first draft showed that it was impossible to develop a low-rise building with a floor space index of 2.5.

As we had to discard our initial plan, we soon realized that a high-rise concept would have to be the answer. Given the location that was finally selected (Takamatsu, Japan, pop. 426,892), the decision to build upwards proved to be the right one, especially regarding issues of urban development. The site is located in a busy, urban high-rise environment; the challenge was to enter into a dialog with the neighboring buildings.

The concept is based on a simple square, leading to a floor space index of 2.5 when stacked. Furthermore, it was important for us to create free space for the building occupants. By simply turning the housing square 12 degrees, we were able to add additional free space capable of being connected to the residential unit. The different sizes of the living spaces (between 45m²-162m²) allow for a resident mix ranging from single persons to extended families. Thanks to the loft-like floor plan, the residents are free to express their creativity and lifestyle as they wish. The flexible furniture leaves enough room for reinterpretations of the living space. The concept also includes a choice of public as well as semi-public open spaces. For example, each tower has a separate level providing room for socialization and communication or for parties in the specially designed "karaoke boxes".

The concept of the entrance level und public open space consists of intersecting building lines, resulting in a pattern that can be used for various purposes (such as sitting, lying, playing, ventilation, natural light for the underground parking lot...) when combined.

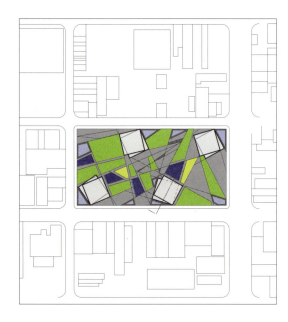

Site

 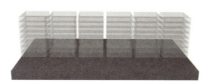 

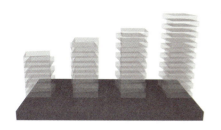  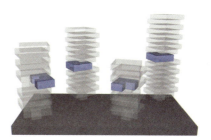

Concept development

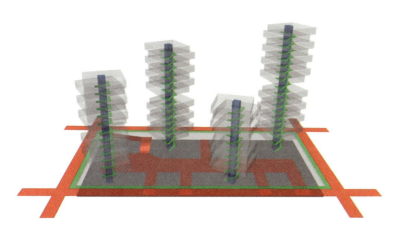 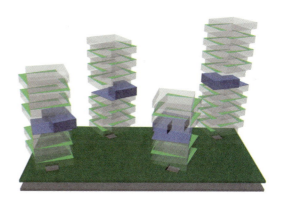

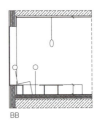
BB

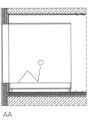
AA

Section
Above: cross section c-c
Below: tower 1

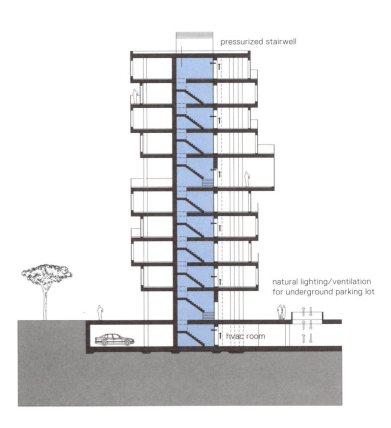

pressurized stairwell

natural lighting/ventilation
for underground parking lot

hvac room

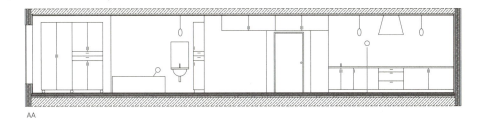

AA

Floor plan
Apartment type 1

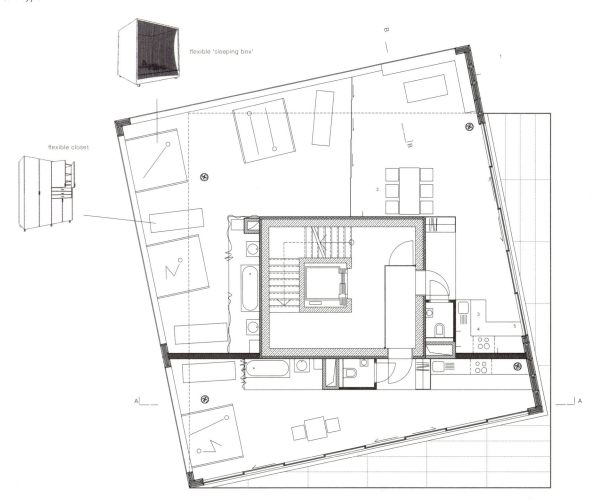

flexible 'sleeping box'

flexible closet

Susanne Fritzer
Instructor

Feyferlik / Fritzer

Wolfgang Feyferlik and
Susanne Fritzer

Founded 1994
Based in Graz

House T
Graz, Austria, 2005

Some thoughts on housing construction and architecture in general.

Realities in Society   The fields of housing and urban development, two areas which are inextricably linked with each other, are currently characterized by a considerable lack of direction. The development of (housing) projects, in which a sensitive adaptation to location and surroundings is a central issue, is a rare exception. Outstanding individual projects (both in a positive and negative sense) do appear from time to time, but only a small number can claim to have a far-reaching concept. The main cause for this is economic pressure, which, as the most important parameter, is given top priority. This pressure also sets the pace, which in turn has a significant (negative) effect on the quality of all project areas (communication, implementation, durability, etc.). Therefore, it is to be hoped that this speed will once again begin to normalize on all levels. Progress has to be seen and understood as a development of societal goals and not merely interpreted as an economic quest and its result. Architecture can be an essential factor and an important "tool" in this process, e.g. in the conservation of resources with respect to energy, required space and the environment in general, as well as in the optimization of public spaces, etc.

Social Challenges   Architecture must be understood [by all parties involved in the project (client – planner – user)] as a long-term process; only then, if it is incorporated in the finding of solutions from the beginning, can it have a positive effect. Life situations change: children are born, grow up, move out; people get older. This is how housing situations change. Architecture should introduce and enable changes and adjustments; especially in the case of housing construction, this should be a crucial concern for all involved.

Ideal Realities   Concepts such as car-free cities, shared spaces and others will remain isolated experiments as long as no broad political will "develops" – judging by the way things are going at the moment, this will still take a long time.

Energy Efficiency   Energy efficiency as a technical parameter, meaning the lowest possible consumption of energy, must become standard. The energy consumption of a building depends primarily on the consumption of every single user and his or her consumption behavior. On the macro level, i.e. for large-scale and/or public-sector projects, this currently means struggling with energy performance indicators. Relevant and unilateral regulations have an increasing influence on architecture and mostly neglect the human factor, with (personal / individual) user behavior and the potential associated with it. Compared to this, there is an increasingly uncritical technization of private households.

Sustainability   A broader education (with respect to energy consciousness) in all areas of life would be the first step towards sustainability, a step which should finally be taken. In general, architecture as a whole should always be seen and treated as a topic implicating sustainability and it should free itself from the influence of short-term trends and tendencies.

Living Density

Annika Hillebrand
Philipp Rudigier
Students

Maria Flöckner
Instructor

Floor space index 2.7

Plot area   5,000 m²
Gross floor area   13,540 m²
Total usable floor space   10,100 m²

Public open space   7,820 m²
Private space   2,844 m²

Housing units   108

Type of construction
Wood construction

Living Density

The concept of the project is based on the idea of a flexible system that reacts to current demographic trends and at the same times leaves room for adaptation to future developments. Ample communication areas (open spaces) are meant to address the issues of housing in old age as well as integration.

The building is located in a densely populated urban area and is bordered by roads in the north and east. Further residential quarters adjoin in the east and west. Structurally, the building establishes a separation from the two roads and forms a quiet and recreational inner courtyard. The ground floor is for the most part elevated on stilts and is used for general public functions such as a supermarket, a mobility center, etc. By opening the ground floor area, the inner courtyard is made accessible to the public and thus becomes an asset for the entire surrounding residential quarter.

In order to reflect the different social identities – no matter if characterized by age, religion, origin, etc. – we chose neutral, flexible floor plans to enable an unhindered individual lifestyle for all residents. The open spaces are combined with the access areas, which results in ample communication areas that can be used by the inhabitants according to their preferences.

The so-called access areas are situated on the ground floor and on the 3rd and 6th floors. These levels are kept almost entirely free of apartments and, in addition to the access, also serve as common open spaces. Apart from the public courtyard area and the semi-public access / open space, there are also communal terraces and private terraces, providing an additional private space for each apartment.

Simple – Fast – Clean

We chose wood as building material because it can be easily used for prefabrication and also because of ecological considerations. All apartments consist of the same modules and, in spite of the variability of the floor plans and diversity of the users, enable a maximum degree of prefabrication. The modules themselves consist of only a small number of different parts and thus facilitate easy planning. The size of the individual "boxes" is determined by the width of the means of transportation, which allows the modules to be assembled in the factory so they just have to be fit together on the construction site. This reduces the construction time (and consequently the costs) to a minimum.

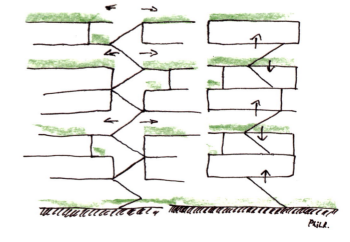

public open space

private open space

public functions

offices, shops

supermarket

playing field

public courtyard

Floor plan ground floor
Above

Diagram access
Left

Section overview
Below

private open space
acess to apartments

staircase

private open space
acess to apartments

staircase

office

private open space
acess to apartments

staircase

private open space
acess to apartments

staircase

private open space
acess to apartments

roof terrace

access level

supermarket

garage

party corner

open space

playground

laundry

staircase

staircase

winter garden

open space

relax area

staircase

staircase

roof terrace

access level

open space

access level

public space

public courtyard

garage

garage

roof terrace

winter garden

access level

function room

Floor plan

First floor (left)
Third floor (right)

Sections

South elevation, b-b (left)
West elevation, a-a (right)

- public open space
- private open space
- public functions
- offices, shops

155

Maria Flöckner
Instructor

maria flöckner und hermann schnöll

Maria Flöckner and
Hermann Schnöll

Founded 1998
Based in Salzburg

House 47°40'48''n / 13°8'12''e
Adnet, Austria, 2007
Temporary rooms

Housing Typologies
Excerpt Introduction Group Maria Flöckner

"Places, places are still there. If a house burns down, it's gone, but the place – the picture of it – stays, and not just in my rememory, but out there, in the world. What I remember is a picture floating around out there outside my head. I mean, even if I don't think it, even if I die, the picture of what I did, or knew, or saw is still out there. Right in the place where it happened." … "If it's still there, waiting, that must mean that nothing ever dies."
    Toni Morrison, Beloved

…The creation of room is always an experimental set-up. There are only indirect ways, only stories about rules or rules for stories. This is the available potential from which the possibilities are derived. You as a student should therefore concentrate on questions like:

What are the demographic developments in our society?

Which groups of people live together in what way, and how do they live alone?

Which cultures live together in what way – migration, symbioses, everyday culture…?

Which observations can you make regarding the immediate physical environement – body studies, motion studies, utilization studies (observe, describe, measure, record) – and which regarding the daily routine?

Which types of motion, rest, perception can you identify and what meaning do they convey?

Which situations can you observe, which combinations – situations of the individual, the couple, the group? Which in private, and which in public space?

Where does life take place? Where is it private and to what extent? Where is it associated with public life? In what places do people stay and for how long? Are there spaces available? Which ones are suitable for what usage?

Examination of threshold spaces – Which ones are adopted and how? How are they used? How could they be used in another way? Which impacts do they have? How are they modifiable? How do they come across in the spatial context?

Which usage overlaps could change which situations? Improve them? Where do you see relations, links, connections? What leads to an extension of the individual body, what to a socialization process?

Try to investigate questions in a state of openness through reflection, observation or examination in day-to-day life. Here, it is necessary to observe closely and document the findings in different forms of presentation. The first model could represent a structure or an atmosphere or a line of thought – the model as an actual image or as the illustration of an idea, an image in the metaphorical sense, so to speak…

Day Care Facility in Taxham
"Living in community"
Taxham, Austria, 2000

Wood on a Higher Level

Isabell Ausserer
Alexandra Stummer
Students

Katharina Fröch
Instructor

Floor space index   2.82

Plot area   5,000 m²
Gross floor area   14,100 m²
Total usable floor space   8,147 m²

Private open space   2,717 m²
Public space   4,750 m²

Housing units   135

Type of construction
Light wood construction on
a reinforced concrete base

 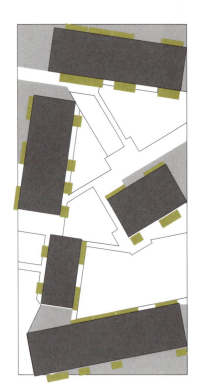 

Open space

Public 2365 m² (40%)
Semi-public 2136 m² (35%)
Private 1418 m² (25%)

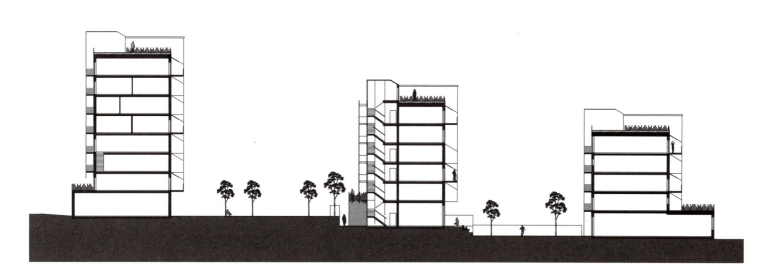

Longitudinal section

Street elevation

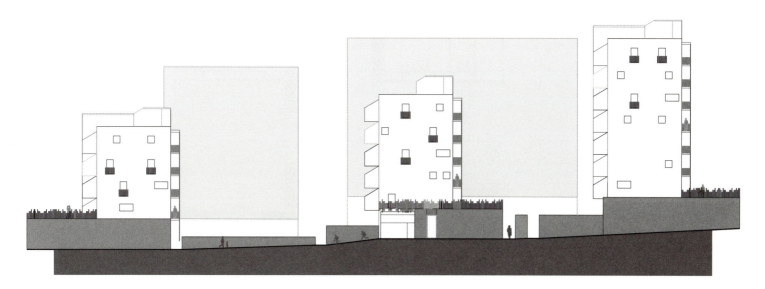

Housing typology

Apartments

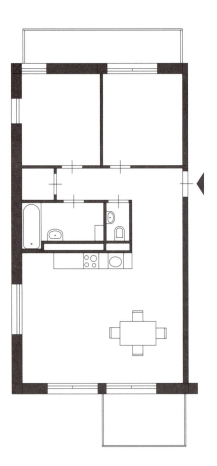

Wood on a Higher Level

What does a floor space index of 3 on 5,000 m² mean? How to deal with this density requirement? How does such a complex influence the urban image, structure and inhabitants?

Our response: A wood frame passive housing estate in the middle of Vienna. It combines a cozy atmosphere with minimal costs for heating and electricity by means of natural materials and its own energy production. The project shows how wood construction fits in with the cultural urban image of Vienna and which advantages it has to offer.

The 100 m long and 50 m wide plot of land is divided into three altitude levels. We used them to arrange the five buildings in such a way as to achieve optimal energy savings. The number of floors is reduced on the southern side. The form strongly resembles a perimeter block development, but there are paths leading directly to the interior of the complex.

The housing estate fosters community life. Open spaces offer room for recreational activities on three levels – the landscaped roof of the ground floor, the communal premises, and the green roofs of the houses. The inhabitants do not focus only on their respective houses, but also make use of the numerous green areas within the housing complex.

The ground floor area is reserved entirely for commerce and community. Nursery school, all-purpose room, library and shops form a convenient link between the estate and the city. Decorative concrete for the ground floor area clearly indicates the separation of the base from the residential building. The shops can be accessed from the street, but at the same time an open view to the interior is provided.

The north and south façades convey a markedly different image. The side facing south is largely dominated by glass, and the façade is characterized by ceiling-high windows, wide balconies with solar panels and additional shading elements. The north façade features steel bars of different lengths, serving as a weather-resisting barrier and additional protruding façade. The majority of the apartments extend through the depth of the building, can be easily extended and have a flexible room layout.

Solar panels with an inclination angle of 30° on the balconies supply the housing complex with power. For this we estimated approximately 1.5 m² of collectors per inhabitant. The apartments are equipped with controlled room ventilation. Water heated by solar energy can be connected directly to the freshwater system.

The solid ground level forms the basis for the reinforced concrete core extending from the basement to the top floor. The wooden rail construction stands on top of the ground level ceiling and is attached to the reinforcing core. The continuous shafts and the massive wooden walls of the structural framework serve as an additional bracing. The structure is composed of wooden rail walls and massive separating walls of cross-laminated wood that can be sustained by supports.

Katharina Fröch
Instructor

Atelier Katharina Fröch

Founded 2006
Based in Vienna

Apartments Vienna 14
Vienna, Austria, 2006

The Individual is Key

The basic motivation of my work is to actively shape the environment and to put people with their needs and necessities at the center of attention.

In the creation of the smallest dimension of form, the living environment, the focus is on the individual with his or her very personal habits. In this process, the objective is always the development of an open floor plan with space as a continuum, as a three-dimensional transformation of the daily routine. The balance between openness and retreat, one of the basic human needs, is given top priority. The conviction of the importance of the haptic and sensorial experience is a major driving force for the choice of visible surfaces and their combination, which contributes to the elaboration of a particular project. As a consequence, there is no uniform personal style in the usual sense. This is part of the concept.

In the next larger dimensions, the shaping of environment with buildings and urban structures, the perspective is shifted towards society. In my view, architecture is always also the image of a society. The urban and rural space we live in influences the way we feel and think. It motivates, stimulates or depresses. Keeping these parameters in mind, analysis is an essential part of the modus operandi for each task. A building does not stand alone; it interacts with the place and its users. It should not follow trends, it can be surprising and it should bear witness to an in-depth analysis of form, space and function.

Penthouse Vienna 4
Vienna, Austria, 2005

Tatami Lounge
Klosterneuburg, Austria, 2008

Cracked

Emeli Steinbacher
Johann Szebeni
Students

Gerda Maria Gerner
Instructor

Floor space index   3

Plot area   5,000 m²
Gross floor area   15,446 m²
Total usable floor space   12,125 m²

Private open space   30,020 m²
Public space   3,320 m²

Housing units   93

Type of construction
Reinforced concrete

Cracked

This residential building is located in Vienna or, alternatively, in one of its suburbs. Our aim was to create an oasis in the city as well as in a more isolated area that is enriching for both inhabitants and neighbors. The building is oriented inwards but at the same time inviting to passers-by. A link to the exterior is formed almost exclusively by the galleries and studios on the ground floor, which gives the building an airy touch and makes it come across as quiet and static, but not overwhelming.

Our main focus of attention was on the open spaces. We offer every inhabitant multiple areas for retreat, such as private terraces in different sizes and forms, a large common terrace, a common garden and a path enlivened by shops, cafés, bakeries and similar facilities. Our rich and varied open space concept, which increases the quality of life and presents manifold opportunities for presentation and production, are perfect for people as ever-changing individuals. The urban approach ensures quiet housing, the conservation of spacious green areas and social sustainability.

The space allocation plan is very complex; every floor plan has a different shape. Even so, the system is clearly recognizable, defined by the line of the paths and the orientation of the apartments. This line was the result of splitting up the high floor space index of 3. We wanted to break this density in the same way that a pothole rips up a street to create and gain new, interesting spaces that make one forget the concentration of the structure.

Our site (which is 85 m long and 58 m wide) is elevated, so the main access is one floor above the galleries and the garage access. We offer electric panel heating because it is generally perceived as the most pleasant type of all heating systems. The 24V low-voltage technique is absolutely safe and allows the heating band to be placed directly under the wall and floor boarding. Just like sunlight, it heats surfaces very consistently and provides pleasant warmth that reaches a comfort level much faster than conventional heating.

Location

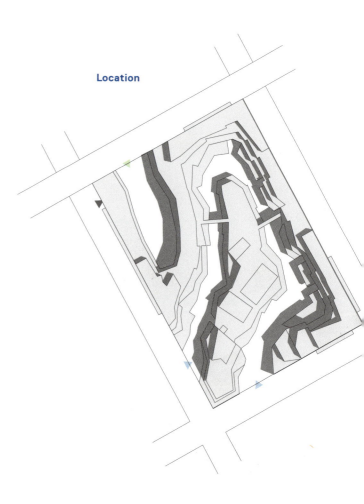

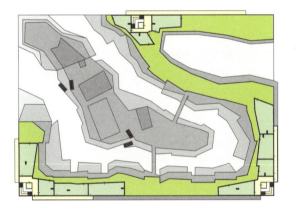

Diagrams

Levels (from above to below)
Left: −1, 0, +1
Right: +2, +3

housing

shops

gallery

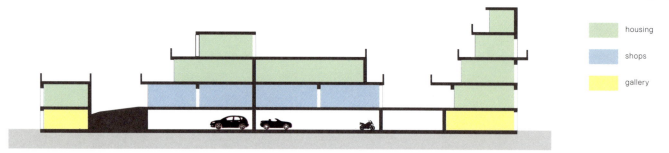

Design approach

- housing
- shops
- gallery

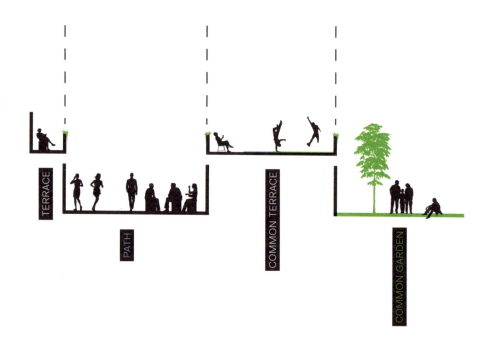

TERRACE

PATH

COMMON TERRACE

COMMON GARDEN

Sections

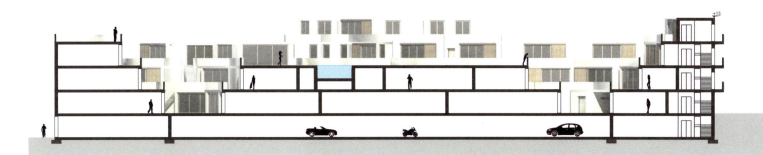

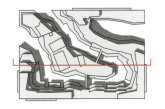

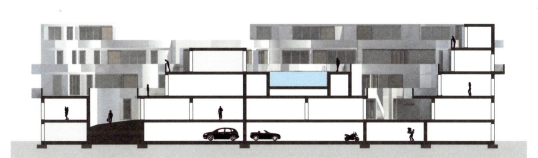

Gerda Maria Gerner
Instructor

gerner°gerner plus

Gerda Maria Gerner and
Andreas Gerner

Founded 1996
Based in Vienna

Residential Building thu
Vienna, Austria, 2008

Residential Building kai
Vienna, Austria, 2005

A Personal Essay on the Topic Housing and Density

A home is individual – ideally, it is custom-made. Who wouldn't like to live in a 6th-floor loft with a view of nature or over water?

Which parameters determine the density (of a city) and how do they influence the inhabitants? Which effects does density have on planning and architecture? How can we as planners nevertheless guarantee the highest architectural quality? What implications does high density have for open space and outdoor environment? A floor space index of 3 – for a plot area of 5,000 m^2 and approximately 15,000 m^2 of usable floor space – for me, this is the most exciting specification. Housing is not only determined by factors such as building regulations, adaptation to the building site, size of the apartments, etc. Social parameters such as opportunities for recreation in a variety of open spaces for all ages and sexes (!), measures for mobility, a choice of rooms without predefined use, etc. have to be taken into account as well, just as the selection of material and construction type should be a matter of course for planning and define architecture.

The dimensions for the predefined, fictitious site were freely selectable – as long as it was not a square. Neither the location of the site nor the inclination should be restricting. I was interested solely in the formation of a high-density housing development in practice, irrespective of surroundings and building regulations, in its implications for housing per se and the resulting possibilities, compromises and experiences.

The result was a range of good solutions. Especially worth mentioning is the selected student project "Cracked" by Emeli Steinbacher and Johann Szebeni, who formed a matrix by cracking the structure open and reached the required density by stacking the obtained material following logical and intelligent considerations. With this landscape, this canyon, they created an amazingly multifaceted quality of housing spaces with a relation to the open spaces. The necessary social open spaces and facilities were integrated in a surprisingly simple and reasonable way or rather emerged automatically owing to the method that was used.

Appendix

Kindly supported by

Federal Chamber of
Architects and Chartered
Engineering Consultants

Chamber of Architects and
Chartered Engineering
Consultants for Vienna, Lower
Austria and Burgenland

Fund for Housing Construction
and Urban Renewal

Cultural Department Science
and Research Promotion

Dean of Admissions for
Architecture and Planning
Programmes, Vienna
University of Technology

Institute of Architecture
and Design, Vienna University
of Technology

Photo credits

AKA77
99
ARTEC Architekten
16 down
Atelier Glück
21, 22 down, 23, 24, 25, 27
Atelier Rainer
32 down, 33, 34 top
Bachlehner, Alfred
11 left
Delthios, Martha
13 right
Ebner, Franz
168,169
Fröch, Katharina
166
Gabriel, Andreas
15 down
Goldgruber, Michael
88, 89
Hilzensauer, Leonhard
58
Hurnaus, Hertha
17 down, 56, 57, 129
Manka, Inge
49 left
Orso, Franziska
106, 107, 109
Ott, Paul
126, 146, 147, 148
PPAG architects
17 top
Rahm architekten
49 right
Rainer, Roland
31, 32 top, 34 down, 36
Rich, Peter
109 down
Rukschcio, Linda
22 top
Russ, Clemens
11 right
Schachinger, Franz
46, 47
Schaller, Lukas
66, 67, 68

Seidl, Manfred
116, 117, 118, 176, 177, 178
Similache Nikolaus
15 top
Stehlik, Ulrike
78
Steiner, Rupert
76, 77, 79, 86, 87
Steixner, Gerhard
Cover, 12, 13 left, 14
Stocker, Gerhard
16 top
Tomaselli, Markus
96, 97
Zenzmaier, Stefan
156, 157, 159

Articles by

Silvia Boday
Marlies Breuss
Eva Češka
Maria Flöckner
Susanne Fritzer
Katharina Fröch
Kinayeh Geiswinkler-Aziz
Gerda Maria Gerner
Feria Gharakhanzadeh
Adele Gindlstrasser
Ulrike Hausdorf
Franziska Orso
Ursula Schneider
Martina Schöberl

**Interviews with Harry Glück
and Roland Rainer**

Excerpts taken from:
*Die Architektur und ich, eine
Bilanz der österreichischen
Architektur seit 1945, vermittelt
durch ihre Protagonisten
[Architecture and me: a review
of Austrian architecture since
1945, as told by its protagonists]*
Editors: Gerhard Steixner,
Maria Welzig, Böhlau Verlag,
Wien 2003